ISBN 978-1-7330564-4-1 (Paper Back)
Book Design and Story by Don Pirozok
Editor Cheryl Pirozok

First Printing 2019 Amazon Publishing, United States

Published By: Pilgrims Progress Publishing
Spokane Valley WA. 99206
Website: www.donpirozok.com

Entrance Into the Kingdom of Heaven

Introduction	Page 4
Chapter 1 The Kingdom of Heaven Is At Hand	Page 23
Chapter 2 Jesus Is the King of the Kingdom	Page 54
Chapter 3 Is Heaven On Earth	Page 71
Chapter 4 The Character of Kingdom Age	Page 98
Chapter 5 Inheriting the Kingdom	Page 109
Chapter 6 Warnings of Kingdom Exclusion	Page 120
Chapter 7 Kingdom Parables	Page 154
Chapter 8 The Kingdom and Judgment Seat	Page 189
Chapter 9 Christian Faith Must Include Next Age	Page 208
Chapter 10 Free Gift and Works of Reward	Page 229
Conclusion	Page 260
Notable Men Who Spoke of Kingdom Exclusion	Page 260
G. H. Lang	Page 260
Pastor B. Herrell	Page 263
Dr. A.B. Simpson	Page 265
Jesse Penn Lewis	Page 266
Robert Govett	Page 267
J.A. Seiss	Page 272
Watchman Nee	Page 276
Albert George Tilley	Page 276
William Frederick Roadhouse	Page 277
Robert Edward Neighbour	Page 278
G. F Ponder	Page 280
Husdson Taylor	Page 282
Barnabus	Page 283
Polycarp	Page 284
Apostle Paul	Page 286

Alfred Taylor Schofield 1846 - 1929

":..we are all perfectly clear that entrance into eternal life is of grace alone...but Scripture clearly shows that there are definite rewards and losses with regard to our Christian conduct in this world....This is the point I would put definitely before you. For forty years I have glossed over every passage which refers to exclusion, and have refused to apply it to the Christian man. But on the face of them, these passages do apply to Christians everywhere. They are in Epistles written to Christians, and are safeguarded at the time, as applying to Christians. I feel that when an Apostle says, 'Be not deceived,' there may be great danger that some will be deceived, in applying Scriptures to other people and carefully shielding the application from ourselves. First, I would appeal to you, on those grounds, quietly to read those short passages which have been alluded to, many of them, over again....'Be not deceived.' Why that solemn warning? No one that is an unconverted adulterer will inherit the kingdom of God. What class then could be deceived? Only Christians....Does not the Apostle bring home to the consciences of Christians (not merely professors or clearly unconverted people to whom these words surely cannot apply), the fact that they shall not inherit the kingdom of God by which I here understood the Millennial Kingdom of Christ?"77*

77*The Entrance Into The Kingdom Of God, Prophecy Investigation Society, Nov. 12th, 1909 (London), 31-32.*

3

Introduction
Kingdom Confusion

Contrary to popular Kingdom of Heaven Theology a lot of confusion has come concerning what the Kingdom of Heaven really is. First in the Lord's Prayer, why should Christians pray for the Kingdom to come, "if it is already here." Why pray for the will of the Lord to be done, if it already is happening? Did you notice the Kingdom has predated the formation of the Church, as it was prepared before the foundation of the world? When Jesus Christ announced the Kingdom of Heaven was at hand, it is the same as saying the Kingdom is near. Why not just say the kingdom of heaven is here? When the Pharisees demanded to know when the Kingdom would come, Jesus Christ said it would come without observation. Even upon the Resurrection of Jesus Christ, the original disciples asked Jesus, "will you at this time restore the Kingdom to Israel." (Acts 1:5) All the Jewish Christians were still looking for the Kingdom in their day, which means it had yet to come.

What is the problem? The modern Church has made the Kingdom of Heaven to mean the Church, and the glory of God spread through the Church all over the world. There are so many problems making the Kingdom the Church, the first being the alarming amount of almost 2000 years of Church corruption. The Kingdom of Heaven is the will of God done on earth with Jesus Christ as the earths King. Jesus Christ warned not everyone who says to Me Lord, Lord will enter the Kingdom of Heaven, but they which do the will of My Father. Let's get real, Church history demonstrates the incredible amount of rebellion to Gods will. Bloodshed by the Catholics in Holy Wars, and Inquisitions enslaving the masses with false doctrines and practices. The Kingdom of Heaven never has been the Catholic Church, or the Pope as it's King.

Next, why would the Scriptures warn Christians can be disqualified from the Kingdom? The Kingdom is to be entered into at the Second Coming of Jesus Christ, some will be shut out. How can the Kingdom be entered into now, and then again at the Second Coming? The Kingdom is also connected to Abraham, Isaac, and Jacob, which would require their resurrection to be a part. The Parables of Talents, Pounds, and 10 Virgins teach Kingdom Age rewards are not given until the Second Coming. Jesus Christ told His apostles they would be given the Kingdom when the Lord would be given the throne of His glory, and the apostles would become immortal, and given 12 thrones to rule with Him.

If we hold to the Scriptures, the Kingdom of Heaven is future at the Second Coming, when the Lord brings the Kingdom with Him. Entrance into the Kingdom requires the resurrection of the righteous dead, an immortal body for the righteous saints. At that time Jesus Christ sits on the Throne of David ruling from the New

Jerusalem as King of the earth. It is at the time of the
Second Coming, the Kingdoms of this world become the
Kingdom of our Lord and His Christ. (Revelation 11:15)
The Kingdom of Heaven is to be entered into at the
return of Jesus Christ, not all who say Lord, Lord will be
qualified to enter, even though born again of the Holy
Spirit.(Matthew 7:21-23) Which proves being saved by
grace, does not guarantee Kingdom of Heaven entrance
by all Christians. Therefore, modern-day Kingdom
Theology can't answer the Scriptures which speak of
Kingdom disqualification, or Kingdom Exclusion for
many Christians.

The Kingdom of Heaven is not given at the new birth,
the born-again experience. The Kingdom of Heaven is
represented as the inheritance, to be given upon
qualifications at the Judgment Seat of Christ. The Cross
of Jesus Christ gives us eternal life, while works of
righteousness done after coming into saving faith are
what qualifies or disqualifies born again Christians from
Kingdom entrance. Christians who are disqualified from
entering the Kingdom, are not sent to Hell. Instead they
have lost their inheritance even though they still
maintain their position of a born-again son of God.
Therefore, Paul warns Christians who continue in the
works of the flesh "will not inherit the Kingdom of God."
(Galatians 5:21) So the Kingdom of Heaven first
proclaimed by Jesus Christ is not yet present and must
be qualified for entrance. At the end of this present age,

the Second Coming, and Jesus Christ physically r
as King on earth.

To make the Kingdom a spiritual birth in our hearts is
inaccurate. Yes, we are born again, and placed in the
Kingdom of the dear Son, with whom we have
redemption in His blood. The sovereign rule of God is a
big part of our lives, His rule as God is certain. However,
the Kingdom of Heaven is very specific, the rule of Christ
on earth with His glorified saints, like Abraham, Isaac
and Jacob. So, the Kingdom of Heaven cannot be a
spiritual kingdom in our hearts, or the sovereign rule of
God now, or already entered and given to Christians.
Instead it is future at the Second Coming, and the
resurrection of the righteous dead into immortality.
Where some Christians will be disqualified and will not
enter the Kingdom of Heaven age.

Matthew 8:10-12
10 When Jesus heard it, he marveled, and said to them
that followed, Verily I say unto you, I have not found so
great faith, no, not in Israel.
11 And I say unto you, that many shall come from the
east and west, and shall sit down with Abraham, and
Isaac, and Jacob, in the kingdom of heaven.
12 But the children of the kingdom shall be cast out into
outer darkness: there shall be weeping and gnashing of
teeth.

Matthew 19:23-30

23 Then said Jesus unto his disciples, Verily I say unto you, That a rich man shall hardly enter into the kingdom of heaven.

24 And again I say unto you, It is easier for a camel to go through the eye of a needle, than for a rich man to enter into the kingdom of God.

25 When his disciples heard it, they were exceedingly amazed, saying, Who then can be saved?

26 But Jesus beheld them, and said unto them, With men this is impossible; but with God all things are possible.

27 Then answered Peter and said unto him, Behold, we have forsaken all, and followed thee; what shall we have therefore?

28 And Jesus said unto them, Verily I say unto you, That ye which have followed me, in the regeneration when the Son of man shall sit in the throne of his glory, ye also shall sit upon twelve thrones, judging the twelve tribes of Israel.

29 And every one that hath forsaken houses, or brethren, or sisters, or father, or mother, or wife, or children, or lands, for my name's sake, shall receive an hundredfold, and shall inherit everlasting life.

30 But many that are first shall be last; and the last shall be first.

Galatians 5:19-21

19 Now the works of the flesh are manifest, which are these; Adultery, fornication, uncleanness, lasciviousness,
20 Idolatry, witchcraft, hatred, variance, emulations, wrath, strife, seditions, heresies,
21 Envyings, murders, drunkenness, revellings, and such like: of the which I tell you before, as I have also told you in time past, that they which do such things shall not inherit the kingdom of God.

Matthew 25:31-34
31 When the Son of man shall come in his glory, and all the holy angels with him, then shall he sit upon the throne of his glory:
32 And before him shall be gathered all nations: and he shall separate them one from another, as a shepherd divideth his sheep from the goats:
33 And he shall set the sheep on his right hand, but the goats on the left.
34 Then shall the King say unto them on his right hand, Come, ye blessed of my Father, inherit the kingdom prepared for you from the foundation of the world:

Separation Unto God

Let's face it, being separated unto the Lord God is an incredibly difficult thing to do. It means death to self, and death to the world. It means picking up the Cross in self-denial daily. It is death to the kingdom of self, making no provision for the flesh, and giving no place to the devil. It's are rare find when one of God's own is completely sold out to live for the Lord rather than self. That saint has gone into the straight gate, and walks in a narrow way, and few are the children of God who have found this.

Abraham is our example of a man, and his family who separated unto the Lord God.

Hebrews 11:8-10
8 By faith Abraham, when he was called to go out into a place which he should after receive for an inheritance, obeyed; and he went out, not knowing whither he went.
9 By faith he sojourned in the land of promise, as in a strange country, dwelling in tabernacles with Isaac and Jacob, the heirs with him of the same promise:
10 For he looked for a city which hath foundations, whose builder and maker is God.

Notice the cost Abraham had to pay, in order to obey God. Abraham had to leave his father, and nation. Now the cost of leaving your father in Middle Eastern culture, was to lose the right of the family inheritance. So, God had promised Abraham an inheritance, but would require Abraham to take his family and go to a land after which Abraham would later receive as an inheritance. Basically, God had promised Abraham the right to inherit the earth, and Abraham's Seed. Abraham obeyed God, and went out away from his Father's blessing, and sojourned in the land of promise.

Abraham for most of his adult life lived in the wilderness, a strange country, dwelling in tents. Abraham had basically a nomadic life, even though Abraham was looking for the city who builder and maker was God. Abraham was looking for God's inheritance and had to live a separated life in order to qualify for God's blessing.

The cost of separation is built upon absolute trust and dependence upon the Lord God. God had promised Abraham a son, but his wife Sarah was barren. Can you imagine the temptation to believe God Had failed you, when your future heirs cannot even be born because your wife is barren? God waited until Abraham was 100 years old, and physically incapable of having children. Sarah's womb was also dead to having children as she was 90, when the son of promise Isaac was born. God's separation process is to break the nature of depending upon human ability, and to put our trust in God's promise and ability.

You might go an entire lifetime without seeing the fulfillment of God's promise in this age. Abraham never saw the fulfillment of God' s promise in his lifetime.

Hebrews 11:13
13 These all died in faith, not having received the promises, but having seen them afar off, and were persuaded of them, and embraced them, and confessed that they were strangers and pilgrims on the earth.

Abraham and his Sarah held on to the promises of God, seeing them afar off, and were convinced to not give up on God. Living a separated life would cost them their convenience. Living as strangers and pilgrims on a journey towards their inheritance. God will give them the land, they will possess the earth as kings and priests, but first would take the promises of God to their graves. It will not be until the first resurrection, when Abraham, Isaac, and Jacob the heirs of God's promised inheritance will raise up from among the dead. To possess the land, to rule they nations of the earth in their immortal bodies. The Kingdom age is all about the meek inheriting the earth. Those who were faithful in their obedience to Jesus Christ, are then qualified for the next as legal heirs, joint heirs with Jesus Christ.

The separated life is costly now and appears foolish to the natural man. However, eye has not seen, nor has ear heard, nor has entered the heart of man what God has prepared for those who love Him. Only true sojourners who have set the eyes upon the Lord, who seek first the coming Kingdom of Heaven, and who did not live for the things of the Gentiles really know the true price of a separated life unto God. For straight is the gate and narrow are the way to the Kingdom, and few are they who find it.

Hebrews 11:8-19

8 By faith Abraham, when he was called to go out into a place which he should after receive for an inheritance, obeyed; and he went out, not knowing whither he went.
9 By faith he sojourned in the land of promise, as in a strange country, dwelling in tabernacles with Isaac and Jacob, the heirs with him of the same promise:
10 For he looked for a city which hath foundations, whose builder and maker is God.
11 Through faith also Sara herself received strength to conceive seed, and was delivered of a child when she was past age, because she judged him faithful who had promised.
12 Therefore sprang there even of one, and him as good as dead, so many as the stars of the sky in multitude, and as the sand which is by the sea shore innumerable.
13 These all died in faith, not having received the promises, but having seen them afar off, and were persuaded of them, and embraced them, and confessed that they were strangers and pilgrims on the earth.
14 For they that say such things declare plainly that they seek a country.
15 And truly, if they had been mindful of that country from whence they came out, they might have had opportunity to have returned.
16 But now they desire a better country, that is, an heavenly: wherefore God is not ashamed to be called their God: for he hath prepared for them a city.

17 By faith Abraham, when he was tried, offered up Isaac: and he that had received the promises offered up his only begotten son,
18 Of whom it was said, That in Isaac shall thy seed be called:
19 Accounting that God was able to raise him up, even from the dead; from whence also he received him in a figure.

God's Sovereign Rule and The Kingdom of Heaven

The earth is the Lord's and the fullness thereof, and they that dwell there in. Why would any question God is in control, His sovereign rule over all? The answer is simple the Kingdoms of this present evil age are in rebellion to God. The world we live in has a system; a governance called the Kingdom of Darkness. The chief ruler is the Prince of the Power of the Air, Satan. Does the Kingdom of Darkness then invalidate the sovereign rule of God over the peoples of the earth, over world history, or over the future of the nations? In no way is the sovereign rule of God diminished at the fall of man, or the formation of nations as all history, and all humanity will be summoned up in Jesus Christ.

Psalm 24:1-2
1 The earth is the Lord's, and the fulness thereof; the world, and they that dwell therein.
2 For he hath founded it upon the seas, and established it upon the floods.

Let's get this right, sin, man's rebellion, Satan and the Kingdom of Darkness cannot alter God at all. No amount of power or ability was lost, none of the will of God has been eliminated. God has intervened on behalf of man in relationship to redemption. God was not caught off guard as if He did not see or know the future, or not see the fall of man, or the rebellion of Satan. The sovereignty of God is not affected by man at all, God determines and then executes His will and no one who has the ability or power to stop Him. Of course, God never acts outside of His character and nature there is no darkness in Him or changing nature. Our Lord God is omniscient, omnipotent, immutable, no other person, or created being has these characteristics.

Psalm 24:3-6
3 Who shall ascend into the hill of the LORD? or who shall stand in his holy place?
4 He that hath clean hands, and a pure heart; who hath not lifted up his soul unto vanity, nor sworn deceitfully.
5 He shall receive the blessing from the LORD, and righteousness from the God of his salvation.
6 This is the generation of them that seek him, that seek thy face, O Jacob. Selah.

Knowing the sovereign rule of God has not diminished with the fall of man, why then did Jesus Christ announce the Kingdom of Heaven? The answer is the Kingdom of Heaven is related to the governance of God among man as an actual government by man. God had promised this kingdom rule to Abraham, and his progeny. The covenant of the Kingdom was given to Abraham, Isaac   15 and Jacob but in their lifetimes, they never experienced its establishment on earth during their lifetimes. This demonstrates the Kingdom of Heaven requires the resurrection of Abraham, Isaac, and Jacob for what God had promised by covenant. Also, God by Covenant promised the Kingdom of Heaven to David, and to David's Son, as David would never lack a son to sit on the Throne of David.

Of course, the Kingdom was never established on earth during the first coming of Jesus Christ. The Roman Empire was never overthrown so the Throne of David, with Jesus Christ as the Son of David ruling from Jerusalem over the nations of the earth was never established. Now we can easily distinguish the Kingdom of Heaven, from the sovereign rule of God. As the Kingdom is an actual kingdom ruled by the Son of David on the Throne of David from the New Jerusalem. This puts the literal rule of Jesus Christ as the King over the nations of the earth at the future Second Coming of Jesus Christ. Never in the minds of the original disciples did they think the Kingdom of Heaven was a spiritual kingdom in their hearts. Or a mystical spiritual kingdom because of their new birth, and the presence of the Holy Spirit. Even upon seeing Jesus Christ resurrected from the dead the original disciples asked Jesus Christ if He was going to "restore the Kingdom to Israel," at that time.

The Scriptures are clear, until the Second Coming the Kingdoms of this world (age), will be in rebellion to God not under the rule of the Kingdom of Heaven. The Kingdom of Heaven is demonstrated to be future by the Scriptures and requires the first resurrection of the saints from the dead with the physical rule of Jesus Christ on earth. At the Second Coming of the Lord is the Battle of Armageddon where the kings of the earth align themselves with Satan and the Antichrist to fight God. When Jesus Christ returns, He comes as the Lord of Hosts to defeat the armies of the Antichrist, and to set up the Kingdom of Heaven on earth. Setting up the Throne of David from the New Jerusalem. It at this time the Kingdoms of this world become the Kingdoms of our God and His Christ.

Revelation 11:15-18
15 And the seventh angel sounded; and there were great voices in heaven, saying, The kingdoms of this world are become the kingdoms of our Lord, and of his Christ; and he shall reign for ever and ever.
16 And the four and twenty elders, which sat before God on their seats, fell upon their faces, and worshipped God,
 17 Saying, We give thee thanks, O Lord God Almighty, which art, and wast, and art to come; because thou hast taken to thee thy great power, and hast reigned.
18 And the nations were angry, and thy wrath is come, and the time of the dead, that they should be judged, and that thou shouldest give reward unto thy servants

the prophets, and to the saints, and them that fear thy name, small and great; and shouldest destroy them which destroy the earth.

19 And the temple of God was opened in heaven, and there was seen in his temple the ark of his testament: and there were lightnings, and voices, and thunderings, and an earthquake, and great hail.

The Kingdom Comes Not with Observation

When Jesus Christ was asked by the religious leadership of His day when the Kingdom of God should come, He answered, "the Kingdom of God comes not with observation." Which makes for an interesting answer for a Jewish culture which knew the Kingdom promised to Israel would be led by the Messiah. The Son of David, their deliverer from foreign army occupation to repossess their land. The Son of David must sit upon the Throne of David and make Israel the head of nations once again. For Jesus Christ to tell the religious leaders they would not be able to see the Kingdom must have been a very disturbing answer.

Next Jesus Christ tells His enemies the Pharisees "the kingdom of God is within you," a completely different set of conditions than what they were looking for. Then later with His disciples Jesus developed more of what they could expect with the coming Kingdom of God. Jesus Christ said, you will desire to see one of the days when the Son of Man (Messiah) will come; "the time of the Kingdom," but you will not see it. In fact, in their lifetime, and for the next 2000 years religious men and women and the Church have been looking for the Kingdom of God on earth. Not even one single day of the Kingdom of God has manifest in 2000 years of Church history. Many in the Church have attempted to redefine what the Kingdom of God really is, as the result of the long delay before the Lord returns with the Kingdom.

Today in the Charismatic Movement it has become fashionable to put the Kingdom label on just about everything being taught. Charismatics have fallen for identifying the Kingdom of God through the Church or by spiritual or mystical experiences. However, none of these teachings or spiritual encounters has made for the Kingdom of God. So according to Jesus Christ when should modern day Christians expect to see the promised Kingdom of God on earth?
"And they shall say to you; see here, or see there, do not go after them, or follow them."
(Luke 17:23)
Why are some many Charismatics chasing what is called the Kingdom of God in Charismatic conferences? The answer is simple; "they follow men who say they see the kingdom," but, are completely blinded by deception.
Jesus Christ said the Kingdom of God is like the lightening shinning in the heavens, and that's how it will come to earth, when the Lord is revealed from heaven

at the Second Coming bringing the Kingdom with Him. Jesus Christ said before the Kingdom, the coming of His crowing on earth must come His rejection of the Cross. Then Jesus Christ said right before the return of the Lord the whole world will be asleep deceived as to the conditions of their day. It will be as in the Days of Noah; all men were living without looking for the coming Judgment of God. Also, the moral state of the world before the coming Kingdom from heaven will be like in the time of Lot in Sodom. In other words, the world will be rejecting the notion of a coming Kingdom age, where Jesus Christ rules the nations of the earth.

Finally, the Lord Jesus warns the Church not to be like Lots wife, unprepared to leave Sodom behind. Jesus Christ warns God will rain down fire this time upon the whole earth like the way He did with Sodom right before Jesus Christ returns to set up the Kingdom on earth. Also, just like Lot and his daughters were delivered from Gods wrath, so in the last days some will be removed from judgment, and others will be left behind to face it. This could possibly be a passage which speaks of a rapture whereby some or all Christians are removed before the judgments of God begin.

The Kingdom of heaven is always taught in Scripture to relate to the Second Coming, and "never before."

Luke 17:20-37

20 And when he was demanded of the Pharisees, when the kingdom of God should come, he answered them and said, The kingdom of God cometh not with observation:

21 Neither shall they say, Lo here! or, lo there! for, behold, the kingdom of God is within you.

22 And he said unto the disciples, The days will come, when ye shall desire to see one of the days of the Son of man, and ye shall not see it.

23 And they shall say to you, See here; or, see there: go not after them, nor follow them.

24 For as the lightning, that lighteneth out of the one part under heaven, shineth unto the other part under heaven; so shall also the Son of man be in his day.

25 But first must he suffer many things, and be rejected of this generation.

26 And as it was in the days of Noe, so shall it be also in the days of the Son of man.

27 They did eat, they drank, they married wives, they were given in marriage, until the day that Noe entered into the ark, and the flood came, and destroyed them all.

28 Likewise also as it was in the days of Lot; they did eat, they drank, they bought, they sold, they planted, they builded;

29 But the same day that Lot went out of Sodom it rained fire and brimstone from heaven, and destroyed them all.

30 Even thus shall it be in the day when the Son of man is revealed.

31 In that day, he which shall be upon the housetop, and his stuff in the house, let him not come down to take it away: and he that is in the field, let him likewise not return back.

32 Remember Lot's wife.

33 Whosoever shall seek to save his life shall lose it; and whosoever shall lose his life shall preserve it.

34 I tell you, in that night there shall be two men in one bed; the one shall be taken, and the other shall be left.

35 Two women shall be grinding together; the one shall be taken, and the other left.

36 Two men shall be in the field; the one shall be taken, and the other left.

37 And they answered and said unto him, Where, Lord? And he said unto them, Wheresoever the body is, thither will the eagles be gathered together.

Chapter 1
The Kingdom of Heaven Is at Hand

Today in the Church the message of the Kingdom of heaven has become a line of demarcation. The debate centers around what the Charismatic Movement calls Kingdom Now, which teaches the Kingdom Age is now. In this doctrinal belief the Charismatic Church will spread the Kingdom of Heaven all over the world before Jesus Christ can return. The rest of the Church either does not look for a coming future Kingdom, (amillennial) or is looking for the Kingdom of Heaven to be set up by Jesus Christ at the Second Coming (Premillennialism). The difference between the two doctrinal beliefs are as far apart as it comes. The Kingdom Now crowd is trying to establish the millennial Kingdom now. As no evidence exists the Kingdom of heaven is now, those who teach on its establishment must use various philosophical beliefs. Christians must discern the truth from error, as all the good intentions of man can never be the substitute for real Bible fact. When it comes right down to it, one must choose who will set up the Kingdom of heaven on earth? The choice is either the Church now, or Jesus Christ at His Second Coming. The Kingdom Now crowd teaches Jesus Christ gave dominion to the Church to spread His Kingdom all over the world before He returns. The premillennial crowd looks for the Kingdom of heaven to come at the Second Coming of Jesus Christ. The Bible teaches only one of these positions. The Scriptures clearly reveal the Lord Jesus Christ transforms the Kingdoms of this present age at the

Second Coming, into the Kingdoms of our God and His Christ.

The final authority and witness must be the Scriptures themselves. The Bible will teach which position is true and the other error. In this book I will say the position of Kingdom future is the only one and true Biblical position. The doctrine is best known as a Premillennial position and is the doctrine of Scriptures. Simply put the Millennial Kingdom, called the Kingdom of Heaven is a future coming kingdom only to be set up at the Second Coming of Jesus Christ.

Let's begin to dissect the Scriptures and breakdown passages on the Kingdom to get their context and meaning. The Scriptures must speak for themselves not being twisted into philosophical beliefs which would corrupt their original intent and meaning. The Bible speaks in plain direct truth with Scriptures confirming other Scriptures, so then the Bible interprets itself. The enemy to doctrine is to twist the Scriptures by allegory, applying symbolic meaning in place of direct literal application. The Bible should be read literally, and where symbols are involved the Bible itself will teach what the symbols mean. Now with keeping Scriptures in the historic context let's see what the Kingdom of heaven is all about.

What Does the Kingdom of Heaven is at hand really mean?

Why did Jesus Christ say the Kingdom of Heaven is at hand? Does this mean the same thing as the Kingdom of heaven has come? Even the Jews knew the Kingdom of heaven must cover the whole earth and must bring righteousness to the world through the Messiah. The Kingdom of heaven would deliver Israel from her enemies, so the Jews were looking for the "Son of David" to deliver Israel from Roman rule and occupation. The Jews knew the Kingdom of heaven on earth would restore Israel under the "rule of God." The difference from announcing the Kingdom is near compared to its actual establishment on earth, ends up being thousands of years later. As the result Jesus Christ always taught the Kingdom of Heaven was future. Now the Charismatics Signs and Wonders Movement have made the practical rule of God on earth in a literal Kingdom to mean something different "a spiritual kingdom." To many Charismatic Christians the Kingdom of heaven has come to mean displays of power, or gifts of healing, prophecy, or even feeling the presence of God in a Charismatic conference. In this way Charismatics say the Kingdom of heaven has come to earth. However, there is a big problem in spiritualizing the actual rule of God on earth, as millennial conditions must exist in the nations. The nations must have God ruling over them in righteous, joy, and peace in the Holy Spirit. To teach the nations are under the rule of God now is sheer ignorance, and even hypocrisy.

The Bible clearly teaches the Kingdoms of this world will act like a beast until the Kingdom of heaven, a stone cut without human aid, comes and strikes the great beast turning it into fine dust. Even now kingdoms of this world are filled with war, terrorism and bloodshed, and the stone is yet to strike the world in judgment.

To spiritualize or allegorize the Kingdom of Heaven making it the Church, or even the Holy Spirit in the hearts of Christians does not make the Kingdom of Heaven now on earth. The rule of God's Kingdom is actual and the realm not symbolic, not allegorical, or spiritual mystical. Therefore, there is a big difference from announcing the Kingdom of Heaven is at hand, and its establishment by the King ruling over the nations. The Signs and Wonders Church is completely off base by hyping up Christians with a super spiritual Kingdom Now theology. No millennial conditions exist now among the nations is just plain fact. The beastly nature of the nations has never been overthrown but the stone from the Mountain of God. The Church has been in existence for almost two thousand years and has never even made one Christian city or nation. When Jesus Christ taught His disciples to pray "your Kingdom Come," it was not a mystical kingdom out of heaven by Charismatic Christians trying to make millennial conditions on the earth through signs and wonders. Instead it is a prayer for the coming Kingdom Age, when Jesus Christ returns with the Kingdom. Jesus Christ brings with Him the Kingdom out of heaven to set up the 1000-year rule of God on earth. At this time the Kingdoms of this world become the Kingdoms of our God and His Christ. Lord let your Kingdom come, Maranatha.

When Jesus Christ was announcing the Kingdom of heaven was at hand, He was declaring the Son of David had come, the King of the Kingdom. Now they rejected their King and Messiah which delayed the restoration of the Kingdom to Israel. It opened the way for Gentiles to be included in the Kingdom Age inheritance. The Cross of Jesus Christ made provision for Gentiles to be grafted into the promises given to Abraham and King David, so theirs could be entrance into the Kingdom too. Christ was announcing He is the promised Messiah the restorer of the Kingdom to Israel, the Son of David. However, their rejection of Messiah caused a delay in the Kingdom which now will be set up at the Second Coming. Until then the Kingdoms of this present age are in rebellion to the rule of God.

Daniel 2:31-45
31 Thou, O king, sawest, and behold a great image. This great image, whose brightness was excellent, stood before thee; and the form thereof was terrible.
32 This image's head was of fine gold, his breast and his arms of silver, his belly and his thighs of brass,
33 His legs of iron, his feet part of iron and part of clay.

34 Thou sawest till that a stone was cut out without hands, which smote the image upon his feet that were of iron and clay, and brake them to pieces.

35 Then was the iron, the clay, the brass, the silver, and the gold, broken to pieces together, and became like the chaff of the summer threshing floors; and the wind carried them away, that no place was found for them: and the stone that smote the image became a great mountain, and filled the whole earth.

36 This is the dream; and we will tell the interpretation thereof before the king.

37 Thou, O king, art a king of kings: for the God of heaven hath given thee a kingdom, power, and strength, and glory.

38 And wheresoever the children of men dwell, the beasts of the field and the fowls of the heaven hath he given into thine hand, and hath made thee ruler over them all. Thou art this head of gold.

39 And after thee shall arise another kingdom inferior to thee, and another third kingdom of brass, which shall bear rule over all the earth.

40 And the fourth kingdom shall be strong as iron: forasmuch as iron breaketh in pieces and subdueth all things: and as iron that breaketh all these, shall it break in pieces and bruise.

41 And whereas thou sawest the feet and toes, part of potters' clay, and part of iron, the kingdom shall be divided; but there shall be in it of the strength of the iron, forasmuch as thou sawest the iron mixed with miry clay.

42 And as the toes of the feet were part of iron, and part of clay, so the kingdom shall be partly strong, and partly broken.

43 And whereas thou sawest iron mixed with miry clay, they shall mingle themselves with the seed of men: but they shall not cleave one to another, even as iron is not mixed with clay.

44 And in the days of these kings shall the God of heaven set up a kingdom, which shall never be destroyed: and the kingdom shall not be left to other people, but it shall break in pieces and consume all these kingdoms, and it shall stand for ever.

45 Forasmuch as thou sawest that the stone was cut out of the mountain without hands, and that it brake in pieces the iron, the brass, the clay, the silver, and the gold; the great God hath made known to the king what shall come to pass hereafter: and the dream is certain, and the interpretation thereof sure.

Antichrist, then Christ, Apostasy, then Millennium

Have you ever noticed how the signs and wonders crowd have made the doctrines of the Second Coming completely backwards? They teach the saving of the world (7 Mountain Gospel) before Jesus Christ can return. They also teach the golden age of the Church before the Second Coming. The improvement of the world, the world getting better all the time, a millennial golden age before the Second Coming. Their message is one of "a glorious Church now," in this present age before the return of Jesus Christ. But one must ask, why would these modern apostles and prophets change the order of events putting them in reverse order? If one simply reads how the apostle Paul lays forth the order of events which must occur before Jesus Christ returns, why teach the direct opposite ordering of events?

1) Paul teaches Antichrist before Jesus Christ
2) Paul teaches apostasy before the Golden age
3) Paul teaches moral decline, before divine ordering and government
4) Paul teaches Church defeat, before the Church conquest
5) Paul teaches Antichrist Kingdom, before Christ's Millennial Kingdom.
6) The Scriptures teach the great Harlot, before the Bride of Christ

Now if any Christian teacher can prove this order of events is false, I will make public correction. However, by the authority of God's Word, the Holy Spirit inspired Paul to lay out how the Kingdom is ushered in. Now we must test why so many in the Charismatic Church teach the reverse the order? Does this not speak of a spirit of error and deception, where false doctrines are treated as true? False doctrines where the truth is maligned and disdained as superstition and unbelief? How can there be such opposing views without a need for great testing of spirits, and teachers?

Where is my proof? Paul's ordering of the events before the Second Coming to the Church of Thessalonians:

1) The day of Christ is always related to the Second Coming
2) That day shall not come until
3) The Great Apostasy of the Church
4) The Man of Sin (Antichrist) revealed
5) The whole world worships and follows the Antichrist
6) Antichrist declares he is God and sits in Jerusalem temple, Abomination of Desolation
7) God removes all restraints which keeps the Antichrist from coming
8) The Lord must sleigh Antichrist with the brightness of His Coming
9) Satanic signs and wonders with the False Prophet calling fire out of heaven
10) Mankind by the millions perish in God's judgment as Antichrist worshipers
11) Strong delusion where mankind believes the Antichrist will bring worldwide
     peace
12) Great Multitudes will follow the Antichrist and blasphemy God
13) The saints which are alive and remain on earth are martyred by Antichrist

Now if these be the order of the facts clearly spelled out by the apostle Paul, where in history has these events even occurred? One must remember the Lord Himself by His literal appearing must destroy the Antichrist. Christian teachers are not given right to make this allegory, myth, or a type. As the bodily physical appearing of the Lord is clearly associated with these events. If the Bible is to be taught as a book of allegory, type, or myth, then nothing can be assured of in Scriptures. Christians could never say the teachings of Jesus Christ are infallible.

The test becomes the for those who teach Kingdom Now allegory, to prove Jesus Christ has already returned bodily in history. I lay for a challenge for any Christian to prove Paul's order of events is not factual, and has already come to past in history already? Here in lies Bible fact, Paul's order of events is infallible, and are yet to be fulfilled in the last days of the Church at the second Coming of Jesus Christ. These days are the Church age and will transition into the Kingdom of Heaven age at the Second Coming.

2 Thessalonians 2:1-12

1 Now we beseech you, brethren, by the coming of our Lord Jesus Christ, and by our gathering together unto him,

2 That ye be not soon shaken in mind, or be troubled, neither by spirit, nor by word, nor by letter as from us, as that the day of Christ is at hand.

3 Let no man deceive you by any means: for that day shall not come, except there come a falling away first, and that man of sin be revealed, the son of perdition;

4 Who opposeth and exalteth himself above all that is called God, or that is worshipped; so that he as God sitteth in the temple of God, shewing himself that he is God.

5 Remember ye not, that, when I was yet with you, I told you these things?

6 And now ye know what withholdeth that he might be revealed in his time.

7 For the mystery of iniquity doth already work: only he who now letteth will let, until he be taken out of the way.

8 And then shall that Wicked be revealed, whom the Lord shall consume with the spirit of his mouth, and shall destroy with the brightness of his coming:

9 Even him, whose coming is after the working of Satan with all power and signs and lying wonders,

10 And with all deceivableness of unrighteousness in them that perish; because they received not the love of the truth, that they might be saved.

11 And for this cause God shall send them strong delusion, that they should believe a lie:

12 That they all might be damned who believed not the truth, but had pleasure in unrighteousness.

Is the Kingdom in Your Heart

Is it right to spiritualize passages of Scripture when the audience being addressed by Jesus Christs teaching were looking at a literal, or factual result? For example, the Pharisee's were looking for the overthrown of the Roman government, and the restoration of Israel to the head of nations. The Pharisees demanded of Jesus Christ when the Kingdom of God should come? The Pharisees' were holding to the Old Testament prophets who foretold of Israel's restoration, after experiencing the judgment of God and the dispersion into the nations (Babylon).

Jesus Christ answered them according to the facts.
1) The Kingdom of God comes not with observation
2) Don't run after people who say here is the Kingdom, or those who proclaim to see it or have   it.
3) The Kingdom of Heaven is in your midst (not in your heart) For the days will come Israel will long to see the Kingdom, the days of the Son of Man, the King of the Kingdom and will "not see it."
4) For as the lightening comes and shines out of heaven so will be the coming of the Son of Man, the King, the Messiah to set up the Kingdom.
5) But first he must suffer many things (Cross) and be rejected as the King of the Kingdom.
6) The time of the coming Kingdom we be as in the days of Noah
7) In the Days of Noah deception will fill the whole earth before God destroyed all but eight souls
8) The Second Coming will also be like the days of Lot and the judgment of Sodom which points to Tribulation before the Kingdom comes.
9) When the Son of Man is revealed, Israel will be in distress, and many Jews will have to flee to the Mountains.
10) God will rescue and remove some faithful from harm's way just like Noah's family and Lots family.

The Scriptures which teach the Kingdom of Heaven is in their midst, in no way means the Kingdom was in the hearts of the Pharisees. In no way do these Scriptures teach the Kingdom of heaven is in the hearts of the Pharisee's spiritually, or anyone else. Instead Jesus Christ gave the factual time of the Kingdom, it would come at the Second Coming and after the Tribulation. Only those who will not take the facts of this teaching would say the Kingdom is in the hearts of believers spiritually. Kingdom Now proponents point out this passage of Scriptures to allegorize or spiritualize the Kingdom.

Why would Jesus Christ say to spiritually dead men, and rebels (Pharisee's) who hated Him, the Kingdom of heaven is in your hearts? You must twist the facts of this passage in order to say Jesus Christ was teaching a kingdom of the heart. What Jesus Christ really taught about the Kingdom in this passage, is at the end of the age just like other passages. The literal Second Coming, and the literal Kingdom overthrowing the worlds control over Israel after thousands of years. Jesus Christ gave the facts when the Kingdom of heaven would be set up in clear facts. Which dozens of Scriptures confirm. Only those who want to spiritualize these passages will twist its true meaning making a false doctrine, the Kingdom of heaven is in the hearts of men spiritually.

Luke 17:20-37
20 And when he was demanded of the Pharisees, when the kingdom of God should come, he answered them

and said, The kingdom of God cometh not with observation:

21 Neither shall they say, Lo here! or, lo there! for, behold, the kingdom of God is within you.

22 And he said unto the disciples, The days will come, when ye shall desire to see one of the days of the Son of man, and ye shall not see it.

23 And they shall say to you, See here; or, see there: go not after them, nor follow them.

24 For as the lightning, that lighteneth out of the one part under heaven, shineth unto the other part under heaven; so shall also the Son of man be in his day.

25 But first must he suffer many things, and be rejected of this generation.

26 And as it was in the days of Noe, so shall it be also in the days of the Son of man.

27 They did eat, they drank, they married wives, they were given in marriage, until the day that Noe entered into the ark, and the flood came, and destroyed them all.

28 Likewise also as it was in the days of Lot; they did eat, they drank, they bought, they sold, they planted, they builded;

29 But the same day that Lot went out of Sodom it rained fire and brimstone from heaven, and destroyed them all.

30 Even thus shall it be in the day when the Son of man is revealed.

31 In that day, he which shall be upon the housetop, and his stuff in the house, let him not come down to

take it away: and he that is in the field, let him likewise not return back.

32 Remember Lot's wife.

33 Whosoever shall seek to save his life shall lose it; and whosoever shall lose his life shall preserve it.

34 I tell you, in that night there shall be two men in one bed; the one shall be taken, and the other shall be left.

35 Two women shall be grinding together; the one shall be taken, and the other left.

36 Two men shall be in the field; the one shall be taken, and the other left.

37 And they answered and said unto him, Where, Lord? And he said unto them, Wheresoever the body is, thither will the eagles be gathered together.

Can Christians Enter the Kingdom Now

Why would the disciples, the Pharisees, and Jesus Christ, all put the Kingdom of Heaven in the future, if the Kingdom of Heaven was already at Hand? The answer is simple, Rome needed to be overthrown and Israel restored to its former greatness like in the days of King David. When Jesus announced the Kingdom was at hand, no Jew took that to mean a spiritual Kingdom in their heart. Instead all Jews believed the Kingdom promised was a literally physical rule of the Son of David. The Messiah ruling from the throne of David from Jerusalem as the head of the nations. Now as a Christian should I now substitute the Church for the Kingdom, and make the Kingdom Now?

The Jews were looking for a literal Kingdom on earth, has the Church now replaced this belief? Let's look at the time when Jesus Christ taught men would enter the Kingdom, now or at His Second Coming.

Does the born-again experience qualify as entrance into the Kingdom? Here are many Scriptures which prove Kingdom of heaven is literal at the Second Coming of Jesus Christ. The Kingdom of Heaven is defined as the 1000-year rule of Jesus Christ from the New Jerusalem at the Second Coming, and after the battle of Armageddon. The throne of David is once again restored, the Son of David (Jesus Christ) sits on David's throne, and Jerusalem is once again the head of all nations. The saints of the first resurrection are all immortal and enter the Kingdom age, and reign with Jesus Christ just like He promised to men like Abraham, Isaac and Jacob.

Failure to enter the Kingdom of heaven at the end of the age is the true warning of Scriptures. Christians are not entering the Kingdom Now through a spiritual birth of the heart. Jesus Christ warns His disciples of not entering the Kingdom in the Sermon on the Mount. Virtually all Scriptures in their plain meaning, taken literally show the Kingdom age to be at the Second Coming of Jesus Christ, and by the resurrection of the righteous dead. As the Kingdom promised to Abraham, Isaac, and Jacob would require their resurrection from the dead. All Scriptures which point to the Kingdom, are future at the Second Coming, and the Resurrection of the Righteous dead. The first resurrection is to be the true timing of entrance into the Kingdom of Heaven. Now the Bible cannot say the Kingdom is Now by the Church, and then say the Kingdom is future at the Resurrection of the righteous dead. Instead all Scriptures taken in their literal face value, do not make the Church the Kingdom of heaven on earth in this age. Instead the Kingdom is literal where Jesus Christ and the resurrected saints rule the nations with a rod of iron. The Bible is clear, the Kingdom of heaven is to be inherited by the saints who qualify for its entrance.

For flesh and blood cannot inherit the Kingdom of God, neither can corruption inherit incorruption. (1 Corinthians 15:50) The Kingdom of Heaven is promised as a future inheritance. The Kingdom of heaven will be given to those who qualify for it by living a righteous holy life in this age. Passages which then give warning of Kingdom forfeiture, warnings given by Jesus Christ and the original apostles about not inheriting the Kingdom of heaven then make sense. Jesus Christ taught His disciples must qualify for its entrance at the end of the age by the first resurrection. Therefore, the Kingdom of heaven is literal at the Second Coming and must be entered at that time.
All other explanations reason away Scriptures and spiritualize or allegorize the Kingdom of Heaven passages to make them twist to fit Kingdom Now philosophy. Even the original disciples who were eyewitnesses to Jesus Christs resurrection did not

believe the Kingdom of heaven was now, and a mystical spiritual kingdom. Instead they asked Jesus Christ at His resurrection a very practical question which was promised by Old Testament prophets; "will you at this time restore the Kingdom to Israel?" (Acts 1:6)

Matthew 8:8-12
8 The centurion answered and said, Lord, I am not worthy that thou shouldest come under my roof: but speak the word only, and my servant shall be healed.
9 For I am a man under authority, having soldiers under me: and I say to this man, Go, and he goeth; and to another, Come, and he cometh; and to my servant, Do this, and he doeth it.
10 When Jesus heard it, he marveled, and said to them that followed, Verily I say unto you, I have not found so great faith, no, not in Israel.
11 And I say unto you, That many shall come from the east and west, and shall sit down with Abraham, and Isaac, and Jacob, in the kingdom of heaven.
12 But the children of the kingdom shall be cast out into outer darkness: there shall be weeping and gnashing of teeth.

Matthew 19:21-30
21 Jesus said unto him, If thou wilt be perfect, go and sell that thou hast, and give to the poor, and thou shalt have treasure in heaven: and come and follow me.
22 But when the young man heard that saying, he went away sorrowful: for he had great possessions.

23 Then said Jesus unto his disciples, Verily I say unto you, That a rich man shall hardly enter into the kingdom of heaven.

24 And again I say unto you, It is easier for a camel to go through the eye of a needle, than for a rich man to enter into the kingdom of God.

25 When his disciples heard it, they were exceedingly amazed, saying, Who then can be saved?

26 But Jesus beheld them, and said unto them, With men this is impossible; but with God all things are possible.

27 Then answered Peter and said unto him, Behold, we have forsaken all, and followed thee; what shall we have therefore?

28 And Jesus said unto them, Verily I say unto you, That ye which have followed me, in the regeneration when the Son of man shall sit in the throne of his glory, ye also shall sit upon twelve thrones, judging the twelve tribes of Israel.

29 And every one that hath forsaken houses, or brethren, or sisters, or father, or mother, or wife, or children, or lands, for my name's sake, shall receive an hundredfold, and shall inherit everlasting life.

30 But many that are first shall be last; and the last shall be first.

Luke 17:20 -30
20 And when he was demanded of the Pharisees, when the kingdom of God should come, he answered them

and said, The kingdom of God cometh not with observation:

21 Neither shall they say, Lo here! or, lo there! for, behold, the kingdom of God is within you.

22 And he said unto the disciples, The days will come, when ye shall desire to see one of the days of the Son of man, and ye shall not see it.

23 And they shall say to you, See here; or, see there: go not after them, nor follow them.

24 For as the lightning, that lighteneth out of the one part under heaven, shineth unto the other part under heaven; so shall also the Son of man be in his day.

25 But first must he suffer many things, and be rejected of this generation.

26 And as it was in the days of Noe, so shall it be also in the days of the Son of man.

27 They did eat, they drank, they married wives, they were given in marriage, until the day that Noe entered into the ark, and the flood came, and destroyed them all.

28 Likewise also as it was in the days of Lot; they did eat, they drank, they bought, they sold, they planted, they builded;

29 But the same day that Lot went out of Sodom it rained fire and brimstone from heaven, and destroyed them all.

30 Even thus shall it be in the day when the Son of man is revealed.

Matthew 7:21-23

21 Not everyone that saith unto me, Lord, Lord, shall enter into the kingdom of heaven; but he that doeth the will of my Father which is in heaven.

22 Many will say to me in that day, Lord, Lord, have we not prophesied in thy name? and in thy name have cast out devils? and in thy name done many wonderful works?

23 And then will I profess unto them, I never knew you: depart from me, ye that work iniquity.

Kingdom Entrance Based Upon First Resurrection

The Scriptures are clear the Kingdom of heaven is future at the Second Coming of Jesus Christ and requires the entrance from the first resurrection. This makes no Christian, or Old Testament saint to have already entered the Kingdom of Heaven age based on being born again or glorified in death. How little has modern theology addressed the vast volume of Scriptures which show entrance into the Kingdom of heaven based upon resurrection and based upon qualification. The apostle Paul has helped clarify the matter of Kingdom entrance based upon resurrection, and glorification into immortality.

1 Corinthians 15:50-55

50 Now this I say, brethren, that flesh and blood cannot inherit the kingdom of God; neither doth corruption inherit incorruption.

51 Behold, I shew you a mystery; We shall not all sleep, but we shall all be changed,

52 In a moment, in the twinkling of an eye, at the last trump: for the trumpet shall sound, and the dead shall be raised incorruptible, and we shall be changed.

53 For this corruptible must put on incorruption, and this mortal must put on immortality.

54 So when this corruptible shall have put on incorruption, and this mortal shall have put on immortality, then shall be brought to pass the saying that is written, Death is swallowed up in victory.

55 O death, where is thy sting? O grave, where is thy victory?

Here are the facts: 1) Flesh and blood cannot inherit the Kingdom of God. Which means your natural birth, or your born-again birth has allowed you to enter the Kingdom. Instead of entrance into the Kingdom in a spiritual birth, Christians are in a journey towards their promised land. At the end of this age all the dead in Christ will be raised from among the dead and judged at the Judgement Seat of Christ. At that time qualification for Kingdom entrance will be determined. Not all who say Lord, Lord shall enter the Kingdom of Heaven, but only those Christians who have done the will of My Father in heaven. The Kingdom is given as reward based upon being faithful to Christ after coming into saving faith. The Cross did not give the Kingdom as a free gift, instead the Kingdom is rewarded to the Sons of God in the first resurrection as a reward of inheritance to "first born sons."

When do the Sons of God appear? At the end of the age at the first resurrection when they put off their mortality for their immortality. Those who qualify for the Kingdom age are like the angels of heaven are immortal and are glorified to wear the crown, and rule from a throne. These are the first-born sons who have attained to the first resurrection as their reward. This is the Church of the first born, those who have qualified in Christ who are raised from the dead into immortality. Upon whom the Second death has no power.

Matthew 22:28-33

28 Therefore in the resurrection whose wife shall she be of the seven? for they all had her.

29 Jesus answered and said unto them, Ye do err, not knowing the scriptures, nor the power of God.

30 For in the resurrection they neither marry, nor are given in marriage, but are as the angels of God in heaven.

31 But as touching the resurrection of the dead, have ye not read that which was spoken unto you by God, saying,

32 I am the God of Abraham, and the God of Isaac, and the God of Jacob? God is not the God of the dead, but of the living.

33 And when the multitude heard this, they were astonished at his doctrine.

Now all who do not attain to the first resurrection cannot enter the Kingdom age. Notice also the second factor 2) Corruption cannot inherit incorruption, so Christians living after the flesh in a corrupted worldly manner will not inherit the Kingdom of God. Blessed and holy are they who partake of the first resurrection. They shall be called the Kings and Priests of our God and shall reign with Him for the 1000-year Kingdom age.

Revelation 20:4-6
4 And I saw thrones, and they sat upon them, and judgment was given unto them: and I saw the souls of them that were beheaded for the witness of Jesus, and for the word of God, and which had not worshipped the beast, neither his image, neither had received his mark upon their foreheads, or in their hands; and they lived and reigned with Christ a thousand years.
5 But the rest of the dead lived not again until the thousand years were finished. This is the first resurrection.
6 Blessed and holy is he that hath part in the first resurrection: on such the second death hath no power, but they shall be priests of God and of Christ, and shall reign with him a thousand years.

Peter Teaches Christians Enter the Kingdom In the Future

First Jesus Christ said, "Not Everyone who says to Me Lord, Lord shall enter the Kingdom of Heaven, but only those who do the will of My Father which is in heaven." (Matthew 7:21) Which many teachers go on to say those who prophesied, and worked miracles, and cast out evil spirits in Jesus name were never really born again because Jesus Christ rejected them at the Judgment Seat; "depart from Me you workers of iniquity." (Matthew 7:23) They say being rejected at the Judgment Seat equals the loss of salvation? However, is it the loss of salvation or the loss of reward? If we compare other Scriptures which warn born again Christians of losing their inheritance at the Judgment, then it would be the loss of reward.

Paul also warns Christians who practice the works of the flesh; "you shall not inherit the Kingdom of God." (Galatians 5:21) Which means you can lose something at the Second Coming of Jesus Christ even if you're a born-again Christian. So, what are some Christians in danger of losing by their fleshly living and conduct right now? Many Christians are not afraid to say salvation can be lost, and those who live Godless lives now can still go to Hell. However, they would struggle with saying Christians would lose the inheritance of the coming Kingdom age. The Scriptures are clear, losing the Kingdom is a very real danger for faithless living in this age. Why would both Jesus Christ and apostles Peter and Paul warn of Kingdom loss if it were not possible for

Christians to lose it? It is apparent the Scriptures teach the entrance into the Kingdom as a right of inheritance given to faithful saints at the end of this age.

The apostle Peter also speaks for a future inheritance for Christians. (1 Peter 1:4) Combined with a salvation ready to be revealed in the last time, which is clearly a future salvation. Now we know Peter already taught Christians are saved by the Cross, so the future reward of inheritance is not automatically given to those saved by the Blood of Atonement. Instead, the inheritance is by qualification, meaning not every born-again Christian will be qualified at the Judgment Seat to receive it. What is this great inheritance reserved for faithful Christians? Simply put the right for Christians to rule with Jesus Christ in the coming Kingdom of Heaven age. Will many Christians lose this right by godless living now? The answer comes through a large volume of passages which warn of Kingdom loss. Peter says it's time for Judgment to begin with the household of God. If the righteous man is scarcely saved, where will the ungodly and sinner appear? (1 Peter 4:18) Does this not demonstrate the difficulty of a future Judgment? Peter then warns of Christians who will not walk in sanctification are become blind and have forgotten they were purged from their former way of life. Peter then warns Christians to make their calling and election sure. For if Christians do the things which are right in the sight of God, they shall never fall? Warning Christians can fall in the coming Judgment. Then Peter concludes his teaching with the promise of future reward for the faithful. What is the reward; "an abundant entrance in the coming Kingdom of our Lord and Savior Jesus Christ." (1 Peter 1:11) Once again the Scriptures loudly proclaim a future kingdom, and future entrance into that Kingdom.

Let's be plainly clear. The Kingdom is future and its entrance future, which the Scriptures warn some Christians will forfeit their entrance. How can the Kingdom be now before the Second Coming, and the Judgment Seat of Christ which qualifies Christians for their entrance?

How seductive is Kingdom Now, as most saints simply believe themselves to be building it through their Churches and ministries right now. But whose kingdom is really being built? Mans or Gods?

2 Peter 1:4-11

4 Whereby are given unto us exceeding great and precious promises: that by these ye might be partakers of the divine nature, having escaped the corruption that is in the world through lust.

5 And beside this, giving all diligence, add to your faith virtue; and to virtue knowledge;

6 And to knowledge temperance; and to temperance patience; and to patience godliness;

7 And to godliness brotherly kindness; and to brotherly kindness charity.

8 For if these things be in you, and abound, they make you that ye shall neither be barren nor unfruitful in the knowledge of our Lord Jesus Christ.

9 But he that lacketh these things is blind, and cannot see afar off, and hath forgotten that he was purged from his old sins.

10 Wherefore the rather, brethren, give diligence to make your calling and election sure: for if ye do these things, ye shall never fall:

11 For so an entrance shall be ministered unto you abundantly into the everlasting kingdom of our Lord and Savior Jesus Christ.

Entrance into Kingdom of Heaven: Now or Future

This might be surprising to modern day Christian theology, Jesus Christ taught entrance into the Kingdom of Heaven at the end of this age. So, if Jesus Christ taught entrance into the Kingdom at the Second Coming, how is it modern day theology places entrance into the Kingdom Now? If we trust the authority of Scriptures, then we must recognize the Bible cannot contradict itself. Either entrance into the Kingdom of heaven is available in this age, or it is not. Entrance into the Kingdom is clearly defined, by Bible fact, not human philosophy, religious beliefs, or Church tradition. So here are the facts:

1) Flesh and blood cannot inherit the Kingdom of God

2) Abraham, Isaac, and Jacob are inheritors which would require their resurrection

3) The Kingdom is promised to the twelve apostles, at the time of the regeneration of this age

4) Not everyone who says Lord, Lord will enter the Kingdom of Heaven

5) If your righteousness does not exceed the righteousness of the Scribes and Pharisees, you will in no wise enter the Kingdom of Heaven

6) If you are a wicked and unprofitable servant, you will be cast into outer darkness outside the Kingdom of heaven.

7) Those who qualify for the Kingdom of heaven neither marry, nor are given in marriage, but are as the angels of heaven (immortal)

8) The Kingdom will not come until after a long delay of the Lord being gone

9) A Servant without the proper wedding attire will be cast outside the Kingdom into the place of the hypocrites.

10)   The Lord has gone into His ascension, and will return with the Kingdom

11)   Paul said Christians who live after the flesh will not inherit the Kingdom of Heaven

12) Those who names are taken out of the Lambs Book of Life cannot enter the Kingdom of Heaven

13) The Thrones of the Kingdom are not set until the overthrow of the Antichrist, and chaining of Satan into the abyss

14) The rule of the earth was promised to Abraham and his progeny, and Abraham was looking for the city whose builder and maker is God. Never saw the promise fulfilled in his lifetime.

15) Many saints died in faith without seeing the promised Kingdom but were seeking a better resurrection living destitute lives for God.

16) The Kingdom is the Theocracy of God established after the stone cut out of the Mountain of God strikes the Kingdoms of the present age and grinds them to fine dust.

17) The Kingdom of God existed before the formation of the world, and existed before the Church

18) Only the sheep are accounted worthy to enter the Kingdom age at the Second Coming of Jesus Christ, while the goats are shut out

19) Jesus Christ told the Pharisees' He was the King of the Kingdom, and the Kingdom would be taken from them and given to a people more deserving.

20) The 12 apostles upon the seeing the resurrection of Jesus Christ asked in Jesus would now at that time restore the Kingdom to Israel.

21) Jesus Christ was declared to be the Son of David, the legal heir to sit upon the Throne of David during the Kingdom age.

These are 21 Scriptural facts which demonstrate the Kingdom of Heaven is still future, is not the Church, must be entered into at the Second Coming of Jesus Christ. Also requires the resurrection of the righteous dead into immortal bodies, and not every Christian who calls Jesus Christ Lord will enter the Kingdom Age.

The Kingdom is not "being born again," as it's just part of the journey towards entrance of the Kingdom at the Second Coming. Also, just because the Kingdom of God is righteous, joy and peace in the Holy Spirit, it does not mean it is a spiritual kingdom in our hearts. A kingdom we have already entered by being born again. This is purely conjecture, stating all Christians who are born again already have entered the Kingdom of Heaven while the Scriptures all point to entrance at the Second Coming. How can Christians fail to enter the Kingdom as warned about in Scriptures, if they have already entered it simply by new birth? It proves the new birth the born-again experience does not guarantee the Kingdom age. As not all Christians will be able to enter it.
(Matthew 7:21-23)

Also, the Kingdom of heaven is not the Church as its predated creation and postdates this age only to be entered at the Second Coming. With all this evidence of Kingdom future why do popular Charismatics say they are bringing the Kingdom of Heaven on earth? It seems the only kingdom their building is one after the own ambition and image.

Chapter 2
Jesus Is the King of the Kingdom

Let's ask a very important question; Is Jesus Christ sitting on His Throne as the King of the Kingdom of heaven?" First let's address the fact Jesus Christ is the King of Kings, but is He the King of the Kingdom Now? In truth Jesus Christ was King before the Cross, many confirmed Jesus was in fact the Son of David the legal heir to the Throne. However, did Jesus Christ acquire the Throne of David? This may surprise many Charismatics, but Jesus Christ has yet to attain to His Kingdom, and yet to sit upon the Throne of David. Currently Jesus Christ functions at the right hand of the Father in Heaven, as the Great High priest, whoever lives to make intercession for us. Jesus Christ is in the in between time of the coming Kingdom age and has not arrived as the King of the Kingdom. This will clear up a lot of confusion among Charismatics who are always attempting to declare the Kingdom of heaven is now. In this way the Kingdom has become a spiritual mystical Kingdom with no need for the actual presence of Jesus Christ on the Earth. However, the Scriptures demonstrate when Jesus Christ takes the Throne, the Kingdoms of this world are in a moments time transformed into the Kingdoms of our God and His Christ. The concept of the Kingdom over thousands of years, or ten thousand of years eventually transforming the earth into the Kingdom of heaven does not exist in reality, or in Scriptures.

Revelation 11:15-19

15 And the seventh angel sounded; and there were great voices in heaven, saying, The kingdoms of this world are become the kingdoms of our Lord, and of his Christ; and he shall reign for ever and ever.
16 And the four and twenty elders, which sat before God on their seats, fell upon their faces, and worshipped God,
17 Saying, We give thee thanks, O Lord God Almighty, which art, and wast, and art to come; because thou hast taken to thee thy great power, and hast reigned.
18 And the nations were angry, and thy wrath is come, and the time of the dead, that they should be judged, and that thou shouldest give reward unto thy servants the prophets, and to the saints, and them that fear thy name, small and great; and shouldest destroy them which destroy the earth.
19 And the temple of God was opened in heaven, and there was seen in his temple the ark of his testament: and there were lightnings, and voices, and thunderings, and an earthquake, and great hail.

When disciples of Jesus Christ are to pray; "your Kingdom Come your will be done on earth as it is in heaven," it is not a prayer for the Church to spread the Kingdom of heaven all over the earth gradually. The Church has been in existence for almost two thousand years, and not one single Christian city or nation has ever been made. The prayer of Your Kingdom Come, instead is a prayer for the Second Coming the return of the King, and the rule of Jesus Christ on earth over the nations. Let's look at the evidence of the coming Kingdom as witnessed by the twenty-four elders in heaven. "You have taken your great power and hast reigned, and the nations were angry..." Did you get that? At the Second Coming at the 7th Trumpet Judgment, Jesus Christ takes His power to rule the nations and they were angry. The time of His wrath is come to subdue all His enemies and reward all His saints.

Now if the Charismatic Church has ears to hear, the King brings the Kingdom with Him. The time of the Kingdom is clearly at the time of regeneration, the resurrection of the righteous dead. Jesus Christ calls the throne of His Kingdom, the Throne of His glory where the nations of the earth bow in complete submission to His rule on earth. Until then the nations are angry, and in rebellion to the Lord. The nations of the earth are beastly in nature ruled by the Prince of the Power of the Air, Satan. In the end the nations of the whole earth align themselves against Jesus Christ and worship the Dragon (Satan) and his false Messiah, Antichrist.

Rule of God; Kingdom Reign

There is a distinct difference with the rule of God as Supreme over all His creation, and Kingdom of Heaven, Jesus Christ's rule on earth. God as the Sovereign

Creator over heaven and earth rules from His Throne in Heaven as all things are determined by the council of His will. God knows the beginning from the end as He is separate from time, and dwells in eternity. The Lord God is the uncreated He never has had a beginning; He will never have an ending. The Supremacy of His preeminence gives Him complete dominion and rule overall. Which includes Satan, all the fallen dark angels, and demon spirits, fallen mankind, and upholding and sustaining all His Universal creation. God dwells in unapproachable light which no man can enter or has seen Him. It is impossible for finite man to take in all "the infinite of God," so God must reveal Himself to us. Men who have been saved by Jesus Christ whose names are written in the Book of Life will never come to know the completeness of God. As it is impossible to put a boundary around the infinite eternal God.

Now the Kingdom of heaven is a different story as it is very specific, as its purpose is the rule and reign of Jesus Christ on earth at the Second Coming. The Kingdom of heaven was promised to Abraham and his seed, where Abraham's progeny would inherit the earth, and rule as King's and Priests in the Kingdom age. In order to fulfill the Blood Covenant promised to Abraham and his seed, Jesus Christ must be made man, be born of a virgin, (God Is Father) and fulfill the terms of the blood Covenant through the sacrificial death on the Cross for our sins. In this way Jesus Christ became the legal heir to David's Throne, the first born from the dead. The Kingdom of heaven requires a resurrection, as flesh and blood cannot inherit the Kingdom of heaven, neither does corruption (sin) inherit incorruption; immortality.(1 Corinthians 15:50) So Abraham, Isaac, and Jacob, must be raised from the dead into immortality in order to rule and reign with Jesus Christ on earth during the Kingdom age.

The Kingdom of Heaven is directly connected to the first resurrection, the Second Coming of Jesus Christ, the New Jerusalem, and Christ's 1000-year rule with the resurrected glorified saints. The Kingdom of heaven was spoken about by the Old Testament prophets in the restoration of Israel and David's son (Jesus Christ) who would bring Israel into the head of all nations once again. When Jesus Christ announced the "kingdom of heaven is at hand;" He was declaring Himself as the prophesied Son of David, who would fulfill the Blood Covenant to Abraham and his descendants. Now the Scriptures reveal in the Kingdom age men will come from the four corners of the world to sit down with Abraham, Isaac and Jacob in the Kingdom of Heaven; but for those who refuse the Christ by burying their talents are in danger of being cast into outer darkness.

So, until the resurrection of the righteous dead no Kingdom of heaven is to be established on earth. The Church is not also the Kingdom of Heaven on earth, as the Kingdom requires the resurrection into immortality. So now the Church can only exercise authority in Jesus name, preach the gospel making disciples of all nations, and prepare for the Second Coming. At which time the

Kingdom of heaven will come to earth, Jesus Christ reigning from the New Jerusalem with His resurrected immortal saints. The last enemy to be put under our feet will be death, and this will happen at the end of the 1000-year rule. After wards Christ delivers up the Kingdom to the Father, and the saints will enter the New Heavens and New Earth age. World without end, no devil, no sin.

Revelation 20
1 And I saw an angel come down from heaven, having the key of the bottomless pit and a great chain in his hand.
2 And he laid hold on the dragon, that old serpent, which is the Devil, and Satan, and bound him a thousand years,
3 And cast him into the bottomless pit, and shut him up, and set a seal upon him, that he should deceive the nations no more, till the thousand years should be fulfilled: and after that he must be loosed a little season.
4 And I saw thrones, and they sat upon them, and judgment was given unto them: and I saw the souls of them that were beheaded for the witness of Jesus, and for the word of God, and which had not worshipped the beast, neither his image, neither had received his mark upon their foreheads, or in their hands; and they lived and reigned with Christ a thousand years.

5 But the rest of the dead lived not again until the thousand years were finished. This is the first resurrection.

6 Blessed and holy is he that hath part in the first resurrection: on such the second death hath no power, but they shall be priests of God and of Christ, and shall reign with him a thousand years.

7 And when the thousand years are expired, Satan shall be loosed out of his prison,

8 And shall go out to deceive the nations which are in the four quarters of the earth, Gog and Magog, to gather them together to battle: the number of whom is as the sand of the sea.

9 And they went up on the breadth of the earth, and compassed the camp of the saints about, and the beloved city: and fire came down from God out of heaven, and devoured them.

10 And the devil that deceived them was cast into the lake of fire and brimstone, where the beast and the false prophet are, and shall be tormented day and night for ever and ever.

11 And I saw a great white throne, and him that sat on it, from whose face the earth and the heaven fled away; and there was found no place for them.

12 And I saw the dead, small and great, stand before God; and the books were opened: and another book was opened, which is the book of life: and the dead were judged out of those things which were written in the books, according to their works.

13 And the sea gave up the dead which were in it; and death and hell delivered up the dead which were in them: and they were judged every man according to their works.

14 And death and hell were cast into the lake of fire. This is the second death.

15 And whosoever was not found written in the book of life was cast into the lake of fire.

The Throne of David

Why is it difficult for modern Christianity to identify the Kingdom of heaven? It was first promised to Abraham and his progeny by God, and by blood Covenant. Let's look at some of the wording: 1) Abraham will be the Father of nations 2) Nations and Kings will come from his lineage 3) The Covenant was established between God, Abraham, and Abraham's seed (Jesus Christ) 4) God gave the land to Abraham, and his seed for an everlasting possession.

The right of rule, to inherit the nations, to rule the earth is connected to the Abrahamic Covenant. So, the Kingdom of Heaven will come from the bloodline of Abraham. The Kingdom was first established by God through David, who was promised by God David would never lack a son to sit upon the Throne of David, forever. Of course, David is in the family line of Abraham, by which Jesus Christ also came from the Tribe of Judah, David's tribe. So, God by Covenant made the Throne of David the everlasting government, the Kingdom which should rule the earth.

Now we can understand why Jesus Christ as the Son of David made proclamation; "the kingdom of heaven is at hand." After the resurrection of Jesus Christ his disciples asked Him, "will you at this time restore the Kingdom to Israel?" His disciples knew the Old Testament prophecies which spoke of God resorting the Kingdom which had fallen after the days of King David, and King Solomon.

Jesus Christ was declaring Himself to be the prophesied Messiah, the Son of David, the legal heir to the Throne of David. None of the Jews thought Jesus Christ was saying He was bringing a spiritual Kingdom to earth which would exist in the hearts of men. The Kingdom was always considered the Theocratic rule of God on earth by Gods King. That's why the Old Testament prophets spoke of its restoration after the destruction of Israel. Let's make this point clear: "Nowhere in Scriptures is the Kingdom of heaven though to be the Church." Neither in Scriptures is the Kingdom said to be a spiritual Kingdom in the hearts of men. Here are the facts: 1) Abraham, Isaac, Jacob must be present in the Kingdom of heaven as it was promised to them by an unfailing Blood Covenant. 2) Only when the Son of David sits on the Throne of David "restoring Jerusalem" as the head of nations will Gods promise to King David be fulfilled. 3) Restoring the Tabernacle of David is about resorting the Kingdom to David's Son. Which requires the government of God to be set up on earth. 4) The Tabernacle of David is where Gods King rules the earth, and is not "replaced by the Church, or worship in the Church."

Jesus Christ told Pilot during His trial His Kingdom was not of this world. (John 18:36) Also which the Book of Revelation confirms, as the Kingdoms of this world become the Kingdoms of our Lord and his Christ at the Second Coming. (Revelation 11:15) When New Testament Scriptures speak of restoration, they speak of God restoring the "theocratic rule of God" on earth by the Kingdom of heaven. The theocratic rule of Jesus Christ the Son of David sitting upon the Throne of David, from the New Jerusalem.

Never has God broken His Covenants to Abraham or King David and replaced the Church in the place where once promised the Kingdom to Israel. Only Christians who refuse the council of Scriptures attempt to put the Kingdom of heaven as the Church, and in this age without the resurrection of Abraham, Isaac, Jacob, and King David. Kingdom Now is pure deception a doctrine of demons corrupting the promises of God making them of non-effect.

Its big denial is to say the beastly kingdoms of the world are being transformed by the Church into the Kingdom of heaven. Just where are the governments of this present age "not in rebellion to God?" The Church has been in existence for almost 2000 years, and never has there be even on single city or nation which has turned into the Kingdom of heaven.

Genesis 17:5-8
5 Neither shall thy name any more be called Abram, but thy name shall be Abraham; for a father of many nations have I made thee.
6 And I will make thee exceeding fruitful, and I will make nations of thee, and kings shall come out of thee.
7 And I will establish my covenant between me and thee and thy seed after thee in their generations for an everlasting covenant, to be a God unto thee, and to thy seed after thee.
8 And I will give unto thee, and to thy seed after thee, the land wherein thou art a stranger, all the land of Canaan, for an everlasting possession; and I will be their God.

2 Samuel 7:8-26
8 Now therefore so shalt thou say unto my servant David, Thus saith the Lord of hosts, I took thee from the sheepcote, from following the sheep, to be ruler over my people, over Israel:
9 And I was with thee whithersoever thou wentest, and have cut off all thine enemies out of thy sight, and have made thee a great name, like unto the name of the great men that are in the earth.
10 Moreover I will appoint a place for my people Israel, and will plant them, that they may dwell in a place of

their own, and move no more; neither shall the children of wickedness afflict them anymore, as beforetime,

11 And as since the time that I commanded judges to be over my people Israel, and have caused thee to rest from all thine enemies. Also the Lord telleth thee that he will make thee an house.

12 And when thy days be fulfilled, and thou shalt sleep with thy fathers, I will set up thy seed after thee, which shall proceed out of thy bowels, and I will establish his kingdom.

13 He shall build an house for my name, and I will stablish the throne of his kingdom forever.

14 I will be his father, and he shall be my son. If he commit iniquity, I will chasten him with the rod of men, and with the stripes of the children of men:

15 But my mercy shall not depart away from him, as I took it from Saul, whom I put away before thee.

16 And thine house and thy kingdom shall be established for ever before thee: thy throne shall be established forever.

17 According to all these words, and according to all this vision, so did Nathan speak unto David.

18 Then went king David in, and sat before the Lord, and he said, Who am I, O Lord God? and what is my house, that thou hast brought me hitherto?

19 And this was yet a small thing in thy sight, O Lord God; but thou hast spoken also of thy servant's house for a great while to come. And is this the manner of man, O Lord God?

20 And what can David say more unto thee? for thou, Lord God, knowest thy servant.

21 For thy word's sake, and according to thine own heart, hast thou done all these great things, to make thy servant know them.

22 Wherefore thou art great, O Lord God: for there is none like thee, neither is there any God beside thee, according to all that we have heard with our ears.

23 And what one nation in the earth is like thy people, even like Israel, whom God went to redeem for a people to himself, and to make him a name, and to do for you great things and terrible, for thy land, before thy people, which thou redeemedst to thee from Egypt, from the nations and their gods?

24 For thou hast confirmed to thyself thy people Israel to be a people unto thee forever: and thou, Lord, art become their God.

25 And now, O Lord God, the word that thou hast spoken concerning thy servant, and concerning his house, establish it forever, and do as thou hast said.

26 And let thy name be magnified forever, saying, The Lord of hosts is the God over Israel: and let the house of thy servant David be established before thee.

Key of David

In the Book of Revelation, Jesus Christ declares He is Holy and true, and has the Key of David. When Christ opens no man can shut or shuts and no man can open. Obviously with the Key of David, Jesus Christ proclaims an ultimate authority which no other man has. Next

Jesus Christ proclaims to the Church of Philadelphia, He has set an open door which no man can shut. The reason this blessing has come upon the Church of Philadelphia is in the face of severe trails and testing the saints had but little strength but held fast their profession of Jesus Christ. This Church is likened unto King David when being chased by King Saul in the wilderness. God had promised David the Throne, but the exact opposite was happening. The life of David was being threatened daily, however, David did not deny God in the time of little power.

Now Philadelphian Christians are given the same promise which was given David the right to rule and reign with Jesus Christ in the coming Kingdom age. The Key of David is connected to the Throne of David, and Gods promise to David, he would never lack for one of David's sons to sit upon the Throne for all eternity. This is called the Davidic Covenant which requires the Lord Jesus Christ to sit upon David's Throne in the New Jerusalem making Israel the head of nations once again. For King David to have Gods promised Kingdom, David himself must be raised from the dead. The sure mercies of David are Gods promise to fulfill all which God has promised to David by blood covenant.

Now Philadelphian Christians in the face of suffering are reminded Jesus Christ has the key. The covenant which was promised to King David, and Jesus Christ as the Son of David was soon to return and sit upon the Throne of

David. The faithfulness of Philadelphian Christians will also qualify them to wear the Crown in the Kingdom age, and to sit upon Thrones ruling and reigning with Jesus Christ. Hold fast which you have, and "let no man take your crown," Let no man deceive and seduce you away from the Kingdom age reward. God will keep you just like He did King David in the hour of your trial and test.

What is the open door, the covenantal promise of the coming Kingdom age the right of entrance because of their faithfulness to Christ now? Philadelphian saints will be rewarded a place in the heavenly city the New Jerusalem, as the Bride of Christ. Is this not what the picture of King David, and his mighty men really represent? A picture of Jesus Christ as the Son of David sitting upon the Throne of David ruling from the New Jerusalem, the Heavenly City with His mighty men the Bride of Christ?

Is not the Key of David connected to the Keys of the Kingdom? The promised future first resurrection for men like Abraham, Isaac, Jacob, and King David to rule and reign with Jesus Christ with immortal glorified bodies? The key which opens the way to the Kingdom was given to Jesus Christ which is the authority of raising the dead. No other man has the power over death, and Hades.

Now why does the modern Charismatic Church fake like spiritual warfare is exercising the Keys of the Kingdom? All the fake casting down of the Devil and fallen dark spirits are just a delusional fantasy of exercising the authority of the Kingdom. The real keys are directly related to power in raising the dead into immortality, and everlasting life only accomplished by Jesus Christ at the Second Coming.

Restoring the Tabernacle of David

Restoration Theology has failed the Charismatic Church by twisting the promises of God given to Israel and attempting to make it fulfilled in the Church. In this case the first century Church is debating with the Pharisaical brothers in Christ who were attempting to say Christians must keep the law after being saved by grace through faith. The apostle James spoke of the restoration of the Tabernacle of David by which the residue of men, and Gentiles who call upon the name of the Lord will seek. In this way apostle James was demonstrating the Church was more than a Church comprised of Jews. The government of God which is coming to the earth can be compared to the restoration of the Tabernacle of David. The time in which the Theocracy of God over the nations was first established through Israel during the times of King David and King Solomon.
The fallen Tabernacle then is the restoration of Gods Theocracy, "after this I will return," meaning the Second Coming of Jesus Christ. Where Jesus Christ as the Son of

David will take the Throne of David and restore Gods Theocratic rule over the nations from the New Jerusalem. Gods promise through the Old Testament Prophets to restore the Kingdom to Israel is directly correlated to the Kingdom of Heaven on Earth. The restoration promised is the Theocratic Kingdom not some missing elements of the Church. The false Charismatic teaching God was speaking of restored apostles and prophets of the Charismatic Movement.

Acts 15:13-18
13 And after they had held their peace, James answered, saying, Men and brethren, hearken unto me:
14 Simeon hath declared how God at the first did visit the Gentiles, to take out of them a people for his name.
15 And to this agree the words of the prophets; as it is written,
16 After this I will return, and will build again the tabernacle of David, which is fallen down; and I will build again the ruins thereof, and I will set it up:
17 That the residue of men might seek after the Lord, and all the Gentiles, upon whom my name is called, saith the Lord, who doeth all these things.
18 Known unto God are all his works from the beginning of the world.

Sadly, Restoration Theology attempts to construct a Kingdom Now theology by the Church and builds a false premise of how God is restoring the Church. A philosophical belief of restored apostles and prophets are now building the true kingdom government in the Church. Instead of the Church being governed by local elders, God is now resorting modern day apostles and prophets in an apostolic wineskin. They say a true Church government which will transform the entire known world before Jesus Christ can return. Of course, this is not the message being taught by the restoration of the Tabernacle of David. Charismatics inventing a pure man-made philosophy attempting to twist the true doctrine of the coming Theocratic Kingdom of Heaven.

Chapter 3
Is Heaven on Earth

Let's get this straight there will never be heaven on earth. Instead the Scriptures speak of a coming Kingdom ruled by Jesus Christ on earth called the Kingdom of Heaven. The Church has absolutely no capacity to bring Heaven to earth. This belief is called a doctrine of demons as it exists nowhere in Scriptures Christians are to bring heaven to earth. Why then has it become so popular in modern day Charismatic Theology? It source comes from a hideous doctrine which makes the Church believe it will take over the world. The Charismatic Super Church will make the nations Christian, their governments Christian before Jesus Christ can return. Do you get that, Jesus Christ cannot return until the Charismatic Super Church has taken over the world making for Christian cities and nations? How is the

Charismatic Super Church to accomplish this task? By bringing heaven to earth according to the Charismatic Super Church apostles and prophets.

Is Gods Throne in heaven coming to earth? Or are Christians seated with God on the Throne? Who will then bring the Government of God to the earth? This is becoming one of the most developed heresies since the false doctrines the Catholic Church fabricated. Declaring Mary to be sinless (Immaculate conception), and God assumed her into heaven soul and body, a false resurrection. (Assumption of Mary) Just because the Church likes to promote popular heresies, does not in any way make them the doctrines of Jesus Christ. The Charismatic Church has come of the rails rejecting the authority of Scriptures, which keep the Church in checks and balances, just like doctrines of demons in Catholicism.

Do you realize a heresy is a sect which is created to draw disciples away from Jesus Christ? Hersey violates the teachings and doctrines of Christ turning men away from following Jesus Christ unto a Movement or a man. It is estimated there are about 1 billion Catholics worldwide who follow the teachings of Catholicism, over against the Scriptures which refute them. It is common for Catholics to pray to Mary as if she holds a position of redeemer. Mary has become a Co redeemer alongside Jesus Christ and has the power to represent Catholics before God. The Catholic Church also wants Catholics to pay indolence's for departed relatives who are in Purgatory. The Bible does not teach an intermediate state by which a man can be saved from venial sins after dying. Also there are thousands of Catholics, likely millions who pray to Mary, who believe the Sacraments are turned into the body and blood of Jesus Christ, (Transubstantiation) and the Priests of Catholicism are the only ones ordained by God to serve the Sacraments.

Now is there any reason to think the Heaven to Earth Charismatic Movement is any less a sect than Roman Catholicism? It matters little to the Movement no doctrines of the Bible teach Christians to bring heaven to earth. Instead like Catholicism where the Pope has authority over the Scriptures, Charismatic Apostles and Prophets declare their "modern revelations" which violate the doctrines of Christ yet are celebrated as the Gospel truth. "Apostolic Popes," who have put their teachings above the Word of God, are now advancing the Heaven to Earth heresy soon to become the largest Protestant Sect in Church history.

It does not matter if the heresy is true or false? Just like Catholic heresy, it's all about the legend which is promoted behind the heresy. Just because Apostolic Protestant Popes say miracles will become without measure, and the Church will spread miracles all over the world making for Christian nations. Does the Bible teach this? What is really behind these Charismatic legends? Charismatic conferences where Christians got drunk in the spirit, feel goose bumps and the hair on their arms stand. Some feathers and gold falling out of thin air, and the "feeling of God" in the atmosphere. Also, some Christians who say they are healed in those meetings, but often have the symptoms of sickness or disease return just after a few days. It's all about the legends created to support the lies and half-truths, and doctrines of demons.

Why do Catholics come running to a piece of toast which has the image of Jesus, or to a statue of Mary which is weeping, or blood coming out of it? Why do Charismatics come running when feathers fall, and gold dust appears? When Charismatics get high and drunk in emotional response "to Gods presence." So, the creators of Charismatic Conferences can say they are "bringing heaven to earth." The Catholics see Mary and receive Messages from her, the Charismatics see angels and receive messages from them. However, both follow doctrines of demons, and can't see the spiritual blindness created by evil spirits.

Why Governments Can't Save the World

Lately, more Christians have come to focus their attention on government, and in some cases are looking for the President to make America great again. Now if the Christian faith we are supposed to pray for our President and nation. In prayer Christians may live peaceable Godly lives not being attacked by our own government because of our commitment to Jesus Christ. However, many Christians are taking government into a philosophical belief, like government can cleanse the nations and bring revival to the world. What is the basic problem with concept of Christian government, or Christian nations? The concept of Church married with government does not exist in the Bible. In Scriptures there is no such concept of a state Church, or a Church of a nation. No concept of an American Church and state, or Church of England or Church of Rome.

Now the government is set into place to theoretically protect its citizens. However, as we see all over the world, governments can be utterly corrupt and evil. Jesus Christ did not attempt to make Rome a Christian nation. Neither did Jesus Christ teach His disciples to preach a social gospel, and reform culture. Instead Jesus Christ called for His disciples to call men out from the Kingdom of darkness which rules over the earth, into the Kingdom of the dear Son, Jesus Christ. Now the disciples were asking Jesus Christ when the "Kingdom of heaven would be restored to Israel?" For the disciples knew if Israel was under Roman domination and rule the Kingdom of heaven was "not yet established." Here in lies a simple fact; the Kingdom of Heaven is a Theocracy, the government and rule of Jesus Christ over the nations. Now if the kingdoms of this present evil age do not have Jesus Christ as their Theocratic King, the Kingdom of Heaven is not in the rule.

Now how long will the Kingdoms of this world rule, before the Theocratic rule of God will be established?

Jesus Christ gave some simple signs by which we could understand the salvation of this world's governments. First, Jesus Christ warned of wars and rumors of wars until the very end of this present evil age. The final worldwide government will be a ten kinged government which upholds the False Messiah as the savior of the world. The Antichrist will rule economically, politically, militarily and require the whole world to worship his image. So here is a simple fact, if the governments of this world exist men will fight and kill one another. Sad to say, God's kingdom will never become the Church government and state government married together to save man from himself in this age.

The only government which arises to rule mankind with religion, and state government is the coming Antichrist government. The end of the age is the most deceptive government of all drawing all men to worship the Antichrist. This will finalize the wrath of God, bringing the judgments of the Book of Revelation upon the kingdoms of this world. Only at the return of Jesus Christ, will the Kingdoms of this world, then become the Kingdoms of our God and His Christ. The Kingdom of Heaven will rule over the Kingdoms of this present age, "by war," called the battle of Armageddon. After the battle led by Jesus Christ and the armies of heaven, the Kingdom of Heaven will be established on earth, as the New Jerusalem. Satan and the powers of darkness will be imprisoned in the abyss. At that time the 1000-year rule of Jesus Christ the Theocratic Kingdom of heaven will begin. "On earth as it is in heaven."

Revelation 19
1 And after these things I heard a great voice of much people in heaven, saying, Alleluia; Salvation, and glory, and honor, and power, unto the Lord our God:
2 For true and righteous are his judgments: for he hath judged the great whore, which did corrupt the earth with her fornication, and hath avenged the blood of his servants at her hand.
3 And again they said, Alleluia. And her smoke rose up for ever and ever.
4 And the four and twenty elders and the four beasts fell down and worshipped God that sat on the throne, saying, Amen; Alleluia.
5 And a voice came out of the throne, saying, Praise our God, all ye his servants, and ye that fear him, both small and great.
6 And I heard as it were the voice of a great multitude, and as the voice of many waters, and as the voice of mighty thunderings, saying, Alleluia: for the Lord God omnipotent reigneth.
7 Let us be glad and rejoice, and give honour to him: for the marriage of the Lamb is come, and his wife hath made herself ready.
8 And to her was granted that she should be arrayed in fine linen, clean and white: for the fine linen is the righteousness of saints.

9 And he saith unto me, Write, Blessed are they which are called unto the marriage supper of the Lamb. And he saith unto me, These are the true sayings of God.

10 And I fell at his feet to worship him. And he said unto me, See thou do it not: I am thy fellow servant, and of thy brethren that have the testimony of Jesus: worship God: for the testimony of Jesus is the spirit of prophecy.

11 And I saw heaven opened, and behold a white horse; and he that sat upon him was called Faithful and True, and in righteousness he doth judge and make war.

12 His eyes were as a flame of fire, and on his head were many crowns; and he had a name written, that no man knew, but he himself.

13 And he was clothed with a vesture dipped in blood: and his name is called The Word of God.

14 And the armies which were in heaven followed him upon white horses, clothed in fine linen, white and clean.

15 And out of his mouth goeth a sharp sword, that with it he should smite the nations: and he shall rule them with a rod of iron: and he treadeth the winepress of the fierceness and wrath of Almighty God.

16 And he hath on his vesture and on his thigh a name written, KING OF KINGS, AND LORD OF LORDS.

17 And I saw an angel standing in the sun; and he cried with a loud voice, saying to all the fowls that fly in the midst of heaven, Come and gather yourselves together unto the supper of the great God;

18 That ye may eat the flesh of kings, and the flesh of captains, and the flesh of mighty men, and the flesh of

horses, and of them that sit on them, and the flesh of all men, both free and bond, both small and great.

19 And I saw the beast, and the kings of the earth, and their armies, gathered together to make war against him that sat on the horse, and against his army.

20 And the beast was taken, and with him the false prophet that wrought miracles before him, with which he deceived them that had received the mark of the beast, and them that worshipped his image. These both were cast alive into a lake of fire burning with brimstone.

21 And the remnant were slain with the sword of him that sat upon the horse, which sword proceeded out of his mouth: and all the fowls were filled with their flesh.

Kingdom of the Cross

In modern day signs and wonders theology power is king. However, In the Bible, the Cross and the fellowship of the sufferings is the Gospel. The world is full of messages of self-improvement, the evolution of man, and human potential. In the Bible the message is no one is good, no one does right, all are fallen, and are natural enemies to God. How are these opposite messages leading fallen mankind, and even effecting the Church? The temptation is for the Church to look powerful and successful in the eyes of the world. That's why business and entertainment run many Churches today, as the Cross looks so completely different than the message of the world. Today the most popular preachers attempt to feed the fallen human nature by teaching our best life is now. While in the Bible the message is pick up the Cross in self-denial, and suffer the loss of all things now, so you can gain the Life of Christ.

The same temptation faces the Church today, as back in the time Jesus Christ first announced the Kingdom of heaven is at hand. The Jews were looking for a powerful world dominating King who would conquer Rome and restore Israel to her greatness. However, their King must look weak, despised, rejected by men, acquainted with sorrow, one whom we hid our faces from in shame. Jesus Christ on the Cross did not look like the conquering King Israel was looking for. Now the Signs and Wonders Church is making the same error. They teach power and kingship is the answer, but the message of the Bible is the Cross for Christians. The most powerful signs and wonders apostles of the first century died humiliating deaths of martyrdom. They were pressed out of measure considered fools of this present age, despised for their commitment to Jesus Christ.

Modern apostles want the Kingdom now, without the price of the death of the Cross. They teach the Charismatics Christians are powerful kings now, spreading the Kingdom of Heaven all over the world without the foolishness of the Cross. However, here is a warning, the Holy Spirit will never anoint the flesh of man, never glorify the worldly ambitions of the Church.

Christian kings are getting their powerful king, but it is not by the Holy Spirit. Just like in the first century the spirit of antichrist attacked the Cross and denied the death of Jesus Christ in the flesh. Now the same temptation is come to Christians to deny any need to crucify their own flesh picking up the Cross in self-denial. The Charismatics teach a Joel's Army is rising in the world. An increase in New Age practices has invaded the Church with soul power and physic ability. New Age practices imitating the work of the Holy Spirit, but glorifying man and not the Lord. Man is ascending to the Throne in the Church, no need to wait for death and resurrection. Just go as a mortal man with soul power and play god. After all the Charismatic apostles teach, we go direct into heaven and sit on the same Throne as Jesus Christ to rule the world as kings for God.

Isaiah 14:5-21
5 The Lord hath broken the staff of the wicked, and the sceptre of the rulers.
6 He who smote the people in wrath with a continual stroke, he that ruled the nations in anger, is persecuted, and none hindereth.
7 The whole earth is at rest, and is quiet: they break forth into singing.
8 Yea, the fir trees rejoice at thee, and the cedars of Lebanon, saying, Since thou art laid down, no feller is come up against us.
9 Hell from beneath is moved for thee to meet thee at thy coming: it stirreth up the dead for thee, even all the

chief ones of the earth; it hath raised up from their thrones all the kings of the nations.

10 All they shall speak and say unto thee, Art thou also become weak as we? art thou become like unto us?

11 Thy pomp is brought down to the grave, and the noise of thy viols: the worm is spread under thee, and the worms cover thee.

12 How art thou fallen from heaven, O Lucifer, son of the morning! how art thou cut down to the ground, which didst weaken the nations!

13 For thou hast said in thine heart, I will ascend into heaven, I will exalt my throne above the stars of God: I will sit also upon the mount of the congregation, in the sides of the north:

14 I will ascend above the heights of the clouds; I will be like the most High.

15 Yet thou shalt be brought down to hell, to the sides of the pit.

16 They that see thee shall narrowly look upon thee, and consider thee, saying, Is this the man that made the earth to tremble, that did shake kingdoms;

17 That made the world as a wilderness, and destroyed the cities thereof; that opened not the house of his prisoners?

18 All the kings of the nations, even all of them, lie in glory, every one in his own house.

19 But thou art cast out of thy grave like an abominable branch, and as the raiment of those that are slain, thrust through with a sword, that go down to the stones of the pit; as a carcase trodden under feet.

20 Thou shalt not be joined with them in burial, because thou hast destroyed thy land, and slain thy people: the seed of evildoers shall never be renowned.
21 Prepare slaughter for his children for the iniquity of their fathers; that they do not rise, nor possess the land, nor fill the face of the world with cities.

Saving the Nations

God's plan from the very beginning was to have the life of Jesus Christ imparted into His created humanity. God gave the original man the right to choose and obey or sin and reject His Word and authority. God foreknew the fall of man, so Jesus Christ is the Lamb of God who was slain before the foundation of the world. God had also planned to have His Son Jesus Christ as the King over all the earth, so made the Kingdom before the foundation of the world. However, through original sin Adam and Eve fell to the kingdom of darkness, and the Prince of the power of the air, Satan who now rules over fallen humanity. The Kingdom is yet to come, neither the rule of Jesus Christ over the nations as the nations are at war with God.

Now with the incarnation of Jesus Christ, God paved the way for the coming Kingdom. Jesus Christ announced the Kingdom of heaven was at hand. The Old Testament prophets had prophesied of the coming Son of David, the Messiah who restores the Kingdom of Heaven to Israel to rule over all the nations of the earth. However, during the time of Christ, the Jews were looking for the immediate appearance of the Kingdom. However, Jesus

Christ warned of the Cross before the Throne. So how does the Lord save the nations of the earth? The Scriptures teach the Kingdoms of this world are saved by the "blood of the Lamb." Just like the deliverance of Israel from Egyptian slavery, and from Pharaoh. By the Blood of the Lamb, the Passover, where God judged the first born of Egypt and brought deliverance. Once again God will judge the nations and divide the sheep from the goats. By the Blood of the Lamb, the Cross of Jesus Christ, and the resurrection of the righteous, Jesus Christ will display the power of the Kingdom at His Second Coming.

Signs and wonders don't save, they only point to the message of Jesus Christ the Lamb of God who was slain, whose blood is the atonement. For without the shedding of the Blood of Jesus Christ there is no reconciliation between God and man. The only thing which stands between the wrath of God, and His judgment on fallen sinful man? The Blood of Jesus Christ. God delivers by the blood covenant, the blood of payment, the blood of atonement, Jesus Christ's blood sacrifice which satisfies God's wrath and justice.

 Now how does the Church get involved in the process? By bringing heaven to earth, and saving the nations of the earth? Of course, this is a "fairy tale," the Church will never save the world as 1500 years of the Catholic Church has demonstrated. Never has even one city, or one nation become "a government of heaven on earth," not even in 1800 years of Christianity. So how does God save the nations; "nothing but the blood of Jesus

Christ." In the end the Lamb who is amid the Throne will open the 7 sealed Book which releases God's end time judgments? Who escapes the judgments of God; "those whose names are written in the Book of Life," and are the Blood bought, "saints of the Lord." The Cross of Jesus Christ has paid for the wrath of God, so the saints do not stand with the unrighteous in judgment.
The Lord will once again judge the world in His righteous, but the blood bought saints have their sins judged already. God will judge the nations, with the 7 sealed Book of Judgment, as seen in the Book of Revelation. (Revelation 5) It is at the Second Coming of the Lord, the nations of the world are judged, and then made into the Kingdoms of our Lord and His Christ. The message of the Church is not signs and wonders transforming the cultures of the world making them Christian before the Lord can return. The heaven to earth message is a "false gospel," bloodless, self-glorying, false kingdom building, antichrist unbelief, undermining of the Cross. False apostles and prophets are preaching a false gospel which undermines the Blood of Jesus Christ. The Charismatic Church is not bringing heaven to earth, neither are the nations being transformed by the Church.

"It's only by the Blood of Jesus Christ, the nations are saved and delivered."

Revelation 5:1-10

1 And I saw in the right hand of him that sat on the throne a book written within and on the backside, sealed with seven seals.

2 And I saw a strong angel proclaiming with a loud voice, Who is worthy to open the book, and to loose the seals thereof?

3 And no man in heaven, nor in earth, neither under the earth, was able to open the book, neither to look thereon.

4 And I wept much, because no man was found worthy to open and to read the book, neither to look thereon.

5 And one of the elders saith unto me, Weep not: behold, the Lion of the tribe of Juda, the Root of David, hath prevailed to open the book, and to loose the seven seals thereof.

6 And I beheld, and, lo, in the midst of the throne and of the four beasts, and in the midst of the elders, stood a Lamb as it had been slain, having seven horns and seven eyes, which are the seven Spirits of God sent forth into all the earth.

7 And he came and took the book out of the right hand of him that sat upon the throne.

8 And when he had taken the book, the four beasts and four and twenty elders fell down before the Lamb, having every one of them harps, and golden vials full of odours, which are the prayers of saints.

9 And they sung a new song, saying, Thou art worthy to take the book, and to open the seals thereof: for thou wast slain, and hast redeemed us to God by thy blood

out of every kindred, and tongue, and people, and nation;
10 And hast made us unto our God kings and priests: and we shall reign on the earth.

Revelation 11:15-19
15 And the seventh angel sounded; and there were great voices in heaven, saying, the kingdoms of this world are become the kingdoms of our Lord, and of his Christ; and he shall reign for ever and ever.
16 And the four and twenty elders, which sat before God on their seats, fell upon their faces, and worshipped God,
17 Saying, We give thee thanks, O Lord God Almighty, which art, and wast, and art to come; because thou hast taken to thee thy great power, and hast reigned.
18 And the nations were angry, and thy wrath is come, and the time of the dead, that they should be judged, and that thou shouldest give reward unto thy servants the prophets, and to the saints, and them that fear thy name, small and great; and shouldest destroy them which destroy the earth.
19 And the temple of God was opened in heaven, and there was seen in his temple the ark of his testament: and there were lightnings, and voices, and thunderings, and an earthquake, and great hail.

The Last Worldwide Empire

Have you ever wondered what the future holds in the last days concerning the nations of the earth? Many in the Church have attempted to predict a Church golden age, a worldwide Christianization of nations. However, several thousands of years ago a man or prayer, the Prophet Daniel, was given a series of visions which detailed the kingdoms of Empires. Which were to rule the earth from the time of Babylon, to Mede/Persian, to Greece, to the Roman Empire in the time of Jesus, and finally, an empire yet formed of the Kingdom of the Antichrist. The final kingdom of the Antichrist will be diverse from any another other worldwide empire before it and stamp all other kingdoms into submission.

Daniel 7:7-11
7 After this I saw in the night visions, and behold a fourth beast, dreadful and terrible, and strong exceedingly; and it had great iron teeth: it devoured and brake in pieces, and stamped the residue with the feet of it: and it was diverse from all the beasts that were before it; and it had ten horns.
8 I considered the horns, and, behold, there came up among them another little horn, before whom there were three of the first horns plucked up by the roots: and, behold, in this horn were eyes like the eyes of man, and a mouth speaking great things.
9 I beheld till the thrones were cast down, and the Ancient of days did sit, whose garment was white as snow, and the hair of his head like the pure wool: his

throne was like the fiery flame, and his wheels as burning fire.

10 A fiery stream issued and came forth from before him: thousand thousands ministered unto him, and ten thousand times ten thousand stood before him: the judgment was set, and the books were opened.

11 I beheld then because of the voice of the great words which the horn spake: I beheld even till the beast was slain, and his body destroyed, and given to the burning flame.

All the worldwide empires are considered by God as beastly in nature. However, the final world empire is different than all others. It is the most beastly of all, dreadful and terrible, and strong exceedingly. Why is this kingdom so different? All other kingdoms had natural men as rulers, the final kingdom has a supernatural man called the Antichrist. Satan comes to earth knowing his time is short and gives his supernatural power to the Antichrist. In addition to Satanic power, the final kingdom has enormous military capacity. By which its military rule can subdue all other nations under it. The world is convinced the Antichrist cannot be destroyed, as the people's say, "who can make war with the Beast"

The whole world follows the final world empire as Satan is openly worshipped. The Antichrist demands all mankind take his mark of worship. Anyone who refuses the Mark of the Beast must go into captivity or is executed. Also, without the Mark of the Beast you cannot buy or sell, so the Kingdom of the Antichrist holds the world's economy too. Never in the history of the world will a Superman hold such power of governance over the face of the earth. The final kingdom is diverse from any other worldwide empires before it, as its leader is the world's false Messiah, the Antichrist.

The Antichrist comes to power in the time of the formation of a ten kinged kingdom and give their allegiance over to the Antichrist. The 10 kings give all their power, and governance to the Antichrist so he emerges as the supreme ruler and dictator of the final world empire. It is during the time of the reign of the Antichrist he makes war with the saints and over comes them for a period of forty-two months. At the end of 3 and ½ years, the Lord Jesus Christ comes with the heavenly army for the final battle of this present age called the Battle of Armageddon. It is in this battle the Antichrist is destroyed. The Antichrist and the False Prophet are judged and placed in the Lake of Fire for the rest of all eternity.

The presence of the Antichrist kingdom does not come into existence until Gods perfect timing. When Gods forces which restrain Antichrist's kingdom are removed, then will the Antichrist and greatest worldwide empire emerge rising from the sea of humanity. God permits the coming of the Antichrist in His timetable, only when the fulness of the Gentiles is complete. The Church will never rule over the Kingdoms of the earth in this age. The Book of the prophet Daniel exposes the lies and deception of false prophets who teach otherwise. When the time comes God sets His thrones and the resurrected saints sit in judgment with God, and God casts the Antichrist kingdom profane from the earth. Like a great burning Mountain cast into the Seas. Or like a great millstone of offense cast profane into the Seas. When the throne of the saints is set by God then the Kingdom of this world become the Kingdoms of His God and Christ. Until then the world is preparing for the coming of the terrible dreadful Beast. For their will be wars, and rumors of wars until then end.

Daniel 7:19-28
19 Then I would know the truth of the fourth beast, which was diverse from all the others, exceeding dreadful, whose teeth were of iron, and his nails of brass; which devoured, brake in pieces, and stamped the residue with his feet;
20 And of the ten horns that were in his head, and of the other which came up, and before whom three fell; even of that horn that had eyes, and a mouth that spake very great things, whose look was more stout than his fellows.
21 I beheld, and the same horn made war with the saints, and prevailed against them;

22 Until the Ancient of days came, and judgment was given to the saints of the most High; and the time came that the saints possessed the kingdom.

23 Thus he said, The fourth beast shall be the fourth kingdom upon earth, which shall be diverse from all kingdoms, and shall devour the whole earth, and shall tread it down, and break it in pieces.

24 And the ten horns out of this kingdom are ten kings that shall arise: and another shall rise after them; and he shall be diverse from the first, and he shall subdue three kings.

25 And he shall speak great words against the most High, and shall wear out the saints of the most High, and think to change times and laws: and they shall be given into his hand until a time and times and the dividing of time.

26 But the judgment shall sit, and they shall take away his dominion, to consume and to destroy it unto the end.

27 And the kingdom and dominion, and the greatness of the kingdom under the whole heaven, shall be given to the people of the saints of the most High, whose kingdom is an everlasting kingdom, and all dominions shall serve and obey him.

28 Hitherto is the end of the matter. As for me Daniel, my cogitations much troubled me, and my countenance changed in me: but I kept the matter in my heart.

Whose Kingdom Now

The Charismatic Church has declared it is their Kingdom Now, but whose Kingdom is now. So, we must ask who oversees the nations of the earth. In Scriptures the Kingdom of this world are described throughout history to have a beastly nature. In comparison to Gods people, the Kingdom of this age are devourers, are hostile to the people of God. This picture of beastly world governments was given to the very end with the most terrible the very last world government. The final government of this age is the Kingdom of the Antichrist aligning itself in a military domination against the people of God. At the heart of the Antichrist Kingdom is the worship of the Devil and his Antichrist. Antichrist worshipers must take a mark called the Mark of the Beast. So prevalent is Satan's temptation to have man worship him in the temptation of Jesus Christ in the wilderness, Satan offered Jesus the Kingdom's of this world if Jesus would just worship him.

Matthew 4:8-10
8 Again, the devil taketh him up into an exceeding high mountain, and sheweth him all the kingdoms of the world, and the glory of them;
9 And saith unto him, All these things will I give thee, if thou wilt fall down and worship me.
10 Then saith Jesus unto him, Get thee hence, Satan: for it is written, Thou shalt worship the Lord thy God, and him only shalt thou serve.

Now when you look at every institution in this age, and you see the same temptation. Satan is offering man to be "his own god," if only man bows down in worship of Satan. Whose Kingdom is it? The Prince who has been given its dominion, the Prince of the Power of the Air, the spirit who now works in the sons of disobedience. This age is called the "present evil age" in Scriptures for a reason. In this world man is always moving according the principle of Babylon, a kingdom of confusion, a worldwide governance of religion and state. Men in this age want to join religion and world government to rule over men. A kingdom without God where mankind is his own Savior. The driving force of Babylon will be to unify the kingdoms of this world under the power of the Antichrist, and a worldwide religion and worship.

Sadly, the Church which has fallen to the world will join league with Babylon. The Great Harlot Church will compromise its worship to God. The Harlot Church will give its worship in the glorification of man and join with the Antichrist government riding the Scarlet Beast. (Revelation 17)

What is the issue with the Great Harlot Church? The Great Whore has committed "fornication with the kings of the earth." This has always been the principle behind Babylon, and now the Harlot Church partakes of the antichrist spirit of Babylon. Is this not the reason for the Catholic Holy Wars, and the Inquisition? Now the Protestant Church is falling to a similar temptation, attempting to rule the nations by Church government.

Fancy new words like "apostolic wineskins," and 7 Mountain Mandate, and Joel's Army. However, the issue is the same, attempting to incorporate Babylon into the Church the unifying of Church and state.

How will it end? Will the Charismatic Church make the Kingdoms of this world the kingdom of heaven? No its just the opposite the Church will be overcome by Satan for a season. The whole world will worship Satan, as the culmination of world history ends in the worship of the Dragon and the false Messiah. The whole world will worship Satan as the final Antichrist kingdom will have all the attributes of the beastly empires before it. However, even more monstrous than all others. "And all who dwell upon the earth shall worship him..." Satan finally establishes his false Messiah and worldwide worship, and the Harlot Church. For what purpose, to have the Kingdoms of this age, "worship Satan now." Now it's easy to see whose Kingdom is Now. Man worships his own image as an indirect way of Satan worship. This world is not the Kingdom of our God, or His Christ. For His reign is the Second Coming where all who worship the Antichrist, and take his mark are cast into the Lake of Fire. Mystery Babylon, the Harlot Church is burnt with fire, and Satan is chained into the abyss. It is at the Second Coming of Jesus Christ the Kingdoms of this present evil age are finally transformed into the Kingdom of heaven.

Until then the Charismatic Church is just being tempted to put the image of man into the sanctuary of God. This is the principle of the Antichrist, and the antichrist spirit.

Man attempting to put his image in place of Jesus
Christ. The proof just listens to all the false apostles who
declare theirs is Kingdom Now.

Revelation 13
1 And I stood upon the sand of the sea, and saw a beast
rise up out of the sea, having seven heads and ten
horns, and upon his horns ten crowns, and upon his
heads the name of blasphemy.
2 And the beast which I saw was like unto a leopard,
and his feet were as the feet of a bear, and his mouth as
the mouth of a lion: and the dragon gave him his power,
and his seat, and great authority.
3 And I saw one of his heads as it were wounded to
death; and his deadly wound was healed: and all the
world wondered after the beast.
4 And they worshipped the dragon which gave power
unto the beast: and they worshipped the beast, saying,
Who is like unto the beast? who is able to make war
with him?
5 And there was given unto him a mouth speaking great
things and blasphemies; and power was given unto him
to continue forty and two months.
6 And he opened his mouth in blasphemy against God,
to blaspheme his name, and his tabernacle, and them
that dwell in heaven.
7 And it was given unto him to make war with the
saints, and to overcome them: and power was given
him over all kindreds, and tongues, and nations.

8 And all that dwell upon the earth shall worship him, whose names are not written in the book of life of the Lamb slain from the foundation of the world.

9 If any man have an ear, let him hear.

10 He that leadeth into captivity shall go into captivity: he that killeth with the sword must be killed with the sword. Here is the patience and the faith of the saints.

11 And I beheld another beast coming up out of the earth; and he had two horns like a lamb, and he spake as a dragon.

12 And he exerciseth all the power of the first beast before him, and causeth the earth and them which dwell therein to worship the first beast, whose deadly wound was healed.

13 And he doeth great wonders, so that he maketh fire come down from heaven on the earth in the sight of men,

14 And deceiveth them that dwell on the earth by the means of those miracles which he had power to do in the sight of the beast; saying to them that dwell on the earth, that they should make an image to the beast, which had the wound by a sword, and did live.

15 And he had power to give life unto the image of the beast, that the image of the beast should both speak, and cause that as many as would not worship the image of the beast should be killed.

16 And he causeth all, both small and great, rich and poor, free and bond, to receive a mark in their right hand, or in their foreheads:

17 And that no man might buy or sell, save he that had the mark, or the name of the beast, or the number of his name.

18 Here is wisdom. Let him that hath understanding count the number of the beast: for it is the number of a man; and his number is Six hundred threescore and six.

Chapter 4
The Character of Kingdom Age

The Millennial Kingdom is the time of Jesus Christ rule on earth from the New Jerusalem. In passages of Scripture identify the Millennium as the time the Kingdom of heaven on earth. This also is the time the prophets of old spoke of the rule of the Messiah over the whole earth.

Isaiah 65: 17-25

17 For, behold, I create new heavens and a new earth: and the former shall not be remembered, nor come into mind.

18 But be ye glad and rejoice for ever in that which I create: for, behold, I create Jerusalem a rejoicing, and her people a joy.

19 And I will rejoice in Jerusalem, and joy in my people: and the voice of weeping shall be no more heard in her, nor the voice of crying.

20 There shall be no more thence an infant of days, nor an old man that hath not filled his days: for the child

shall die an hundred years old; but the sinner being an hundred years old shall be accursed.

21 And they shall build houses, and inhabit them; and they shall plant vineyards, and eat the fruit of them.

22 They shall not build, and another inhabit; they shall not plant, and another eat: for as the days of a tree are the days of my people, and mine elect shall long enjoy the work of their hands.

23 They shall not labour in vain, nor bring forth for trouble; for they are the seed of the blessed of the Lord, and their offspring with them.

24 And it shall come to pass, that before they call, I will answer; and while they are yet speaking, I will hear.

25 The wolf and the lamb shall feed together, and the lion shall eat straw like the bullock: and dust shall be the serpent's meat. They shall not hurt nor destroy in all my holy mountain, saith the Lord.

Notice the change of conditions in the millennial kingdom age. First, after the Lord has brought His catastrophic judgments in the Tribulation, the heavens and earth of old are transformed. A New heavens and New Earth along with a New Jerusalem usher in the Millennial age. Israel is restored as the head nation over all other nations. Jesus Christ is sitting upon the throne of His glory, the Throne of David, ruling the nations with a rod of iron from the New Jerusalem.

Life has been dramatically altered by the presence of the Lord on earth. As the knowledge of the glory of the Lord will cover the earth as the waters cover the sea.

The life span of man is dramatically altered. A man dying at one hundred years of age will be considered young. So, death is still present at the beginning of the Millennial age. However, at the end of the one thousand year rule the last enemy death is finally put away.

Also, the nature of animals has changed, and the predatory nature is greatly altered. The wolf and the lamb shall feed together, and the lion shall eat straw like the bull or cow. Satan has been chained in the abyss, so the nations are free from demonic presence, and warfare with evil spirits. They shall not hurt of destroy in all my holy mountain. No wars, no rumors of wars, the spears have been beaten into plow shears. They shall not plant, and another eat. For the curse over the whole earth has been greatly altered, and finally death itself will be completely defeated. Deaths dominion will put fully under the Lord and placed into the final judgment.

This is just one of many dozens of Old Testament passages which the prophets of Old spoke by inspiration of the Holy Spirit. Prophetic words given as promises to Gods kingdom age saints. In the Jewish mind the concept of the Kingdom was firmly established by the prophets. So, when Jesus Christ announced the Kingdom of heaven was at hand, there was no confusion as to its announcement. Instead the battle was over Jesus Christ as the Son of David, and the legal heir to the Throne of David.

Saints Must Qualify to Rule with Christ

Christians can qualify to rule with Jesus Christ in the Kingdom of heaven age. You are in a race to finish the course to win a prize, an imperishable crown. Paul called the prize of the high calling the right to rule and reign with Jesus Christ in the next age. Paul said if he did not bring his body into subjection, he would be disapproved, a reprobate, one not qualified. Now was Paul to be cast away from his salvation, after having suffered so much for the faith? Absolutely not, Paul was speaking of not obtaining the Crown, being disqualified at the Judgment Seat of Christ not qualifying for Kingdom of Heaven age right to rule.

1 Corinthians 9:24-27
24 Know ye not that they which run in a race run all, but one receiveth the prize? So run, that ye may obtain.
25 And every man that striveth for the mastery is temperate in all things. Now they do it to obtain a corruptible crown; but we an incorruptible.
26 I therefore so run, not as uncertainly; so fight I, not as one that beateth the air:
27 But I keep under my body, and bring it into subjection: lest that by any means, when I have preached to others, I myself should be a castaway.

The prize of the high calling is the right of being crowned. A King Priest, an immortal saint, who qualifies for the first resurrection obtaining the Kingdom age as a qualified son of God. Many today in the modern Church attempt to boast of a crown they have not yet attained, and a kingship in which they have no throne. Many Christians are attempting to display an authority, and power which demonstrates they are already kings in this present evil age. As the result of the lack of true kingship, all manner of "prophetic decrees," are made to declare their false kingship, and kingdom. Others display fantasy spiritual warfare games, even holding court in heaven to bring Satan to trial. They have "invented practices" which are not the true government of God. They are not kings seated upon heavenly thrones executing the government of God throughout the earth. Their kingdom is one of the flesh, self-declared, a religious game, which refuses to pick up the Cross in self-denial fellowshipping in the sufferings of Christ. They are in effect disqualifying themselves by not running "legally," they have yet to finish the race, yet want to declare the prize of the victor.

The Crown and Throne of the Kingdom is not given until the end of the age. To this purpose Jesus Christ was abundantly clear. Jesus Christ said the throne the right to rule in the Kingdom age would only be given to those saints who were willing to pay full price now. You must surrender all to Jesus Christ now in authentic devotion, committing all to Him in service willing to count all things lost. This is what Jesus Christ meant when He commanded His disciples to "seek first the Kingdom, and His righteousness."

Matthew 19:27-30

27 Then answered Peter and said unto him, Behold, we have forsaken all, and followed thee; what shall we have therefore?

28 And Jesus said unto them, Verily I say unto you, That ye which have followed me, in the regeneration when the Son of man shall sit in the throne of his glory, ye also shall sit upon twelve thrones, judging the twelve tribes of Israel.

29 And every one that hath forsaken houses, or brethren, or sisters, or father, or mother, or wife, or children, or lands, for my name's sake, shall receive an hundredfold, and shall inherit everlasting life.

30 But many that are first shall be last; and the last shall be first.

Peter was seeking the Kingdom the right to rule with Jesus Christ, however before then Peter was required to give all to Jesus Christ. "Behold we have forsaken all, and followed you, what shall we have therefore?" (Matthew 19:27). In the regeneration, and the time which Christ returns the coming transformation into the Kingdom age, "when the Son of Man shall sit in the Throne of His glory," (future event), you (Peter) shall be rewarded with "your own Throne." (Future) For today is the day of qualification, and everyone who has forsaken houses, brothers, sisters, or fathers, or mothers, or wife, or children, or lands, for the sake of Jesus Christ shall inherit the Crown and Throne. For the Kingdom age is given by inheritance only to the qualified.

Now comes the true recognition of Jesus Christs warning; not everyone who says to Me Lord, Lord shall enter the Kingdom of heaven. For many will come to Me on that day (Day of Judgment) and say to Me Lord did we not prophesy in your name, in your name work mighty miracles, and in your name cast out evil spirits? I will say to you "depart from Me you workers of iniquity..." These Christians attempted to win the Crown by taking the things of God and using them for themselves. They did not run the race in a lawful way and were disqualified from the crown. All their pretense play acting as if they were great kings failed them at the Judgment. It cost them the real Crown and Kingdom Age Throne. Imposters and pretenders who are "being crowned by manmade glorification," have their "reward now." A perishable crown of man's glory, which is quickly fading, disqualifying them for the next age. Fake kings now with manmade self-serving kingdoms.

Charismatics Who Teach Worldwide Conquest

Let's face it the conditions which exist worldwide today are hostile to the Christian faith. As the Bible describes the salvation of the nations, the transformation of the nations into the Kingdom of Heaven, Christians must understand how the saving of the nation's comes about. The time recognized by Scriptures as a transformed world is connected to the rule of God on earth. So how much power and ability does the Church have to transform the nations into a Christian government the rule of God on earth?

Right now, this question is of vital importance as the Charismatic Movement has said the Church has been given the Commission by God to make the nations, the governments of this present age into the Kingdom of Heaven on earth. Without question in the most prominent teachers of the Apostolic/Prophetic Charismatic Movement is the doctrinal belief the Church is the agency which makes for the Kingdom of Heaven on Earth. To put this simply, the Church must subdue the Kingdom of Darkness as it exists today, put Satan and evil spirits under the dominion of the Church, and transform government and cultures of the nations into a Christian world. Anything less than complete submission and domination of evil empires, or demonic influences is not what the Bible describes as the rule of God on earth in the Kingdom of Heaven.

If the Church is going to abide by the authority of Scriptures Satan and evil spirits must be crushed by the Kingdom of Heaven. Satan must be subdued and placed in chains in the abyss, so Satan's authority over the nations is eliminated. All this destruction of Satanic rule is what is described as the Kingdom of Heaven on earth. The Charismatics who believes the Church has been given the authority to bring the Kingdom on earth and spread it all over the world call the process of Christianizing the nations the 7 Mountain Mandate. The commitment to teach the 7 Mountain Gospel is very real by apostles of the Charismatics who teach the Church is saving the nations. Charismatics who are committed to this belief also frequently speak of great international revivals which will sweep through the nations transforming their population and cultural influences into Christian populations, and Christian culture. Make no mistake the doctrines of a worldwide Church take over by the Charismatics are foundational.

Now let's look at the current progress of Charismatics making the nations of the earth into the Kingdom of Heaven. At this time there is not one single nation or city where the transformation of government, or culture has made the Kingdom of Heaven on earth. Of course, the Church has been in existence for almost two thousand years, and the Catholic Church was the first to claim it was the Kingdom of Heaven on earth. As the Roman Catholic Empire set out to conquer the world by military might, and domination over culture by religious rule as the Kingdom of Heaven. The Roman Catholics were the first to declare the doctrine of Pre-Millennialism as heresy and banned it from the Church. For the first three hundred years the first century Church and Christians taught the Kingdom of Heaven on earth would be established by Jesus Christ Himself, a doctrine called Premillennialism. Jesus Christ Himself would engage in war with Satan and the hostile nations of the earth in an end time battle called the Battle of Armageddon. Jesus Christ would bring the Kingdom of Heaven on earth at the Second Coming, defeat Satan and instantly transform the nations into the Kingdom of Heaven on earth setting up His throne on earth from the New Jerusalem.

Charismatics teach the Church over hundreds of years by mighty miracles will transform the nations gradually making for the Kingdom of heaven on earth. As no nation or city has ever become the Kingdom of Heaven, great prophetic predictions of an international revival must be believed as the evidence the Church is accomplishing the salvation of the world. Or you can clearly see all this belief is simply a lie which has no basis, or support of Scriptures. Is in fact a deception by Satanic spirits which are corrupting the authority of Scriptures, a practice called doctrines of demons. Taught by ignorant apostles and prophets who have led the Church on a wild goose chase attempting to build a religious kingdom out of Church government. Whose manmade philosophies are seducing entire generations into Satanic deception. Open your eyes and give an account to your "nonexistent worldwide Church take over." American apostles and prophets are not even able to transform America which is currently in its greatest departure from Jesus Christ, and Bible ethics this nation has "ever seen." America is becoming a godless secular nation, open your eyes and quit deceiving the Church and yourselves. No Church, or Charismatic Movement has ever had the ability to make the world Christian. We can only preach the Gospel of the Kingdom, and wait for the King to bring the

Kingdom, Jesus Christ Himself saves the world at the Second Coming. The King and Kingdom arrive at the same time, and the nations of the earth are instantly transformed into the Kingdom of Heaven on earth as the King takes His throne in visible rule on earth.

Jesus Christ is the conqueror of the earth, not Charismatic apostles who are self-deceived. The true of the Kingdom as taught by the written Word of God. Scriptural facts taken from hundreds of Scriptures who teach the true doctrine of the Kingdom of Heaven on Earth.

Revelation 11:15-19
15 And the seventh angel sounded; and there were great voices in heaven, saying, The kingdoms of this world are become the kingdoms of our Lord, and of his Christ; and he shall reign for ever and ever.
16 And the four and twenty elders, which sat before God on their seats, fell upon their faces, and worshipped God,
17 Saying, We give thee thanks, O Lord God Almighty, which art, and wast, and art to come; because thou hast taken to thee thy great power, and hast reigned.
18 And the nations were angry, and thy wrath is come, and the time of the dead, that they should be judged, and that thou shouldest give reward unto thy servants the prophets, and to the saints, and them that fear thy name, small and great; and shouldest destroy them which destroy the earth.

19 And the temple of God was opened in heaven, and there was seen in his temple the ark of his testament: and there were lightnings, and voices, and thunderings, and an earthquake, and great hail.

Chapter 5
Inheriting the Kingdom

The Kingdom of Heaven Given as Inheritance

Why would Jesus Christ announce the Kingdom, and then warn His apostles many who call Him Lord would not enter the Kingdom of Heaven? Also, the apostle Paul warned sinning Christians which practice works of the flesh will not "inherit the Kingdom of God?" In this way the Scriptures seem to contradict themselves, is the Kingdom now or later? Also are we in the Kingdom by spiritual birth, or do we inherit it later? These are good questions which must be thoroughly examined by Scriptures. So here are the facts: 1) Not all who call Jesus Christ Lord will enter the Kingdom of Heaven. In fact, may on the Day of Judgment will say to the Lord; we prophesied in your name, worked miracles, and cast out evil spirits. Yet the Lord will say to them, "depart from Me you workers of iniquity." (Matthew 7:21-23)

This verse proves entrance into the Kingdom is at the Second Coming after the judgment of the saints, and not every Christian will qualify. Jesus Christ told His disciples unless your righteousness exceeds that of the

Scribes and Pharisees, they would in no wise enter the Kingdom of Heaven. This of course would not mean the righteousness given by the Cross, as acceptance before God and forgiveness of sins is already given as the free gift of grace. Instead is the practical righteousness of Christian who lives in obedience after coming into saving faith. The Kingdom cannot be entered into as a "free gift," simply by being born again. Instead it can be lost or rewarded to the born again by righteous or unrighteous living. It is to be rewarded as an inheritance at the end of this age to saints who by Godly lives will qualify for its reward.

The apostle Paul confirms the Kingdom is still the future and can be lost or gained by the saints after coming into saving faith. Paul warned Christians those who live after the flesh are in danger of forfeiting their future inheritance and will lose the right to enter the Kingdom age. The writer of the Book of Hebrews also warns of Kingdom forfeiture just like Israel who tempted God ten times in the wilderness were shut out of their inheritance at the end of their journey. God warns Christians not to be like Israel seeing they could not enter the Promised Land because of an evil heart of unbelief in departing from the Living God. In other words, Israel led by the presence of God after their deliverance from Egyptian slavery, and by the Passover Blood of the Lamb could not guarantee their entrance into the Promised Land. Instead those who rebelled died in the wilderness outside their inheritance. God then warns Christians they too can fail to enter the rest at the end of the age. "Beware brethren" lest there be found in you an evil heart hardened by the deceitfulness of sin. In the same ways Paul gives many warning passages of being disinherited and being shut out from Kingdom age entrance. All these passages warn Christians about not inheriting the Kingdom of Heaven age.

Can I as a born-again believer by unrighteous conduct in this lifetime be disqualified at the Judgment Seat of Christ? Be rejected by Jesus Christ at the Judgment Seat? Rejected from obtaining the inheritance of the promised rest at the end of this age? Can I be like Esau who for a single carnal meal sell out my birthright for the pleasures of sin? Most Christians have been taught the Kingdom is automatically given, but this is not how the Scriptures read.

1 Corinthians 6:7-11
7 Now therefore there is utterly a fault among you, because ye go to law one with another. Why do ye not rather take wrong? why do ye not rather suffer yourselves to be defrauded?
8 Nay, ye do wrong, and defraud, and that your brethren.
9 Know ye not that the unrighteous shall not inherit the kingdom of God? Be not deceived: neither fornicators, nor idolaters, nor adulterers, nor effeminate, nor abusers of themselves with mankind,

10 Nor thieves, nor covetous, nor drunkards, nor revilers, nor extortioners, shall inherit the kingdom of God.

11 And such were some of you: but ye are washed, but ye are sanctified, but ye are justified in the name of the Lord Jesus, and by the Spirit of our God.

Galatians 5:13-21

13 For, brethren, ye have been called unto liberty; only use not liberty for an occasion to the flesh, but by love serve one another.

14 For all the law is fulfilled in one word, even in this; Thou shalt love thy neighbor as thyself.

15 But if ye bite and devour one another, take heed that ye be not consumed one of another.

16 This I say then, Walk in the Spirit, and ye shall not fulfil the lust of the flesh.

17 For the flesh lusteth against the Spirit, and the Spirit against the flesh: and these are contrary the one to the other: so that ye cannot do the things that ye would.

18 But if ye be led of the Spirit, ye are not under the law.

19 Now the works of the flesh are manifest, which are these; Adultery, fornication, uncleanness, lasciviousness,

20 Idolatry, witchcraft, hatred, variance, emulations, wrath, strife, seditions, heresies,

21 Envyings, murders, drunkenness, revellings, and such like: of the which I tell you before, as I have also told

you in time past, that they which do such things shall not inherit the kingdom of God.

Ephesians 5:1-7
1 Be ye therefore followers of God, as dear children;
2 And walk in love, as Christ also hath loved us, and hath given himself for us an offering and a sacrifice to God for a sweet smelling savour.
3 But fornication, and all uncleanness, or covetousness, let it not be once named among you, as becometh saints;
4 Neither filthiness, nor foolish talking, nor jesting, which are not convenient: but rather giving of thanks.
5 For this ye know, that no whoremonger, nor unclean person, nor covetous man, who is an idolater, hath any inheritance in the kingdom of Christ and of God.
6 Let no man deceive you with vain words: for because of these things cometh the wrath of God upon the children of disobedience.
7 Be not ye therefore partakers with them.

What Does It Mean to Be Disinherited by God

With the Church many want to discuss if a Christian can lose their salvation or not. In Scriptures the dialogue is around being "disinherited after coming into saving faith." Jesus Christ warned of the loss of the Kingdom of Heaven by speaking of Christians being disinherited.

Matthew 5:19-20
19 Whosoever therefore shall break one of these least commandments, and shall teach men so, he shall be called the least in the kingdom of heaven: but whosoever shall do and teach them, the same shall be called great in the kingdom of heaven.
20 For I say unto you, That except your righteousness shall exceed the righteousness of the scribes and Pharisees, ye shall in no case enter into the kingdom of heaven.

An inheritance comes from the family treasure after the death of the mother and father. After death the passage of family goods are given to the next generation of relatives who are given the inheritance by birth right. So true inheritors of Scriptures are "first born sons." However, can be forfeited by unrighteous living like Esau who lost the right of the first-born son, and Isaac was given the right of inheritance of the first-born son. In Scriptures Gods inheritance is the Kingdom of Heaven given to those who qualify as first-born sons at the end of this present evil age. The inheritance of God is the right to enter the Kingdom of Heaven to rule and reign the nations as Kings and Priests with Jesus Christ. To be disinherited as a Christian is to be kept out from entering the Kingdom in the next age. Instead of the loss of salvation the Scriptures speak of Christians being disinherited from the coming Kingdom age.

Even in the Old Testament God spoke of disinheriting those who sinned in the wilderness journey by shutting them out of the promised land at the end of their journey.

Numbers 14:10-12
10 But all the congregation bade stone them with stones. And the glory of the Lord appeared in the tabernacle of the congregation before all the children of Israel.
11 And the Lord said unto Moses, How long will this people provoke me? and how long will it be ere they believe me, for all the signs which I have shewed among them?
12 I will smite them with the pestilence, and disinherit them, and will make of thee a greater nation and mightier than they.

In the New Testament the subject of being disinherited by being shut out of the Kingdom Age rest from all our enemies is written. Once again, those saints of God who rebel and sin against God with an "evil heart of unbelief," are kept out of the coming inheritance. The comparison is with the nation of Israel in the wilderness which could not enter the promised land because of sin against God.

Notice the warning of failing to enter Gods rest at the end of this age is compared to sinning Israel's saints who failed to enter the promised land. God warns blood bought Christians not to have an evil heart of unbelief which would shut out born again Christians from inheriting the Kingdom age. The Bible says take heed "brethren" meaning brothers in Christ, lest there be found in you an evil heart of unbelief hardened by the deceitfulness of sin. In this way a sin hardened Christian is compared to those of Israel who failed to enter their promised land because of sin.

This is the true meaning of Christians being disinherited, "shall not inherit the Kingdom of Heaven."

Galatians 5:19-21
19 Now the works of the flesh are manifest, which are these; Adultery, fornication, uncleanness, lasciviousness,
20 Idolatry, witchcraft, hatred, variance, emulations, wrath, strife, seditions, heresies,
21 Envyings, murders, drunkenness, revellings, and such like: of the which I tell you before, as I have also told you in time past, that they which do such things shall not inherit the kingdom of God.

Hebrews 3:7-19
7 Wherefore (as the Holy Ghost saith, To day if ye will hear his voice,
8 Harden not your hearts, as in the provocation, in the day of temptation in the wilderness:
9 When your fathers tempted me, proved me, and saw my works forty years.

10 Wherefore I was grieved with that generation, and said, They do always err in their heart; and they have not known my ways.

11 So I sware in my wrath, They shall not enter into my rest.)

12 Take heed, brethren, lest there be in any of you an evil heart of unbelief, in departing from the living God.

13 But exhort one another daily, while it is called To day; lest any of you be hardened through the deceitfulness of sin.

14 For we are made partakers of Christ, if we hold the beginning of our confidence stedfast unto the end;

15 While it is said, To day if ye will hear his voice, harden not your hearts, as in the provocation.

16 For some, when they had heard, did provoke: howbeit not all that came out of Egypt by Moses.

17 But with whom was he grieved forty years? was it not with them that had sinned, whose carcases fell in the wilderness?

18 And to whom sware he that they should not enter into his rest, but to them that believed not?

19 So we see that they could not enter in because of unbelief.

Judgments of Kingdom Rewards or Loss

Matthew 25:34
34 Then shall the King say unto them on his right hand, Come, ye blessed of my Father, inherit the kingdom prepared for you from the foundation of the world.

What are the facts of this passage: 1) A separation of sheep from the goats at the Second Coming. 2) Only the blessed of the Father inherit the Kingdom 3) The Fathers blessing was given to the sons of God who were qualified at the Coming of the Lord. 4) The Kingdom of Heaven existed before the formation of man, and was "only given to qualified sons at the end of the age." 5) This fits with Jesus Christs warning in Matthew 7; Not everyone who says to Me Lord, Lord shall enter the Kingdom of Heaven, but "only those who do the will of My Father in heaven." 6) This matches with other passages of Scripture warning of Kingdom forfeiture.

Galatians 5:21
21 Envyings, murders, drunkenness, revellings, and such like: of the which I tell you before, as I have also told you in time past, that they which do such things shall not inherit the kingdom of God.

The possibility of born-again Christians not inheriting the Kingdom of Heaven at the end of this age is very real. The Scriptures teach the Kingdom is given only to qualified Sons of God. Who by reason of their faithful devotion and pursuit of the will of God are qualified at the Judgment Seat of Christ to inherit the Kingdom? Now Esau is an example in Scriptures of a "first born son" who sold his birth right the right of inheritance (the Fathers blessing, and kingdom), for the things of this present evil age. On the other hand, Jacob, the second born, wrestled with God and man to obtain the right of the first born, and the Fathers inheritance.

Now for the challenge just what exactly is the meaning; "You shall not inherit the Kingdom?" From the onset I want to say the Scriptures teach Kingdom forfeiture, and failure for Christians to not enter the Kingdom of heaven. You have your "works tested," not your salvation. Salvation is not put through the fire, only the quality of material based upon works, gold, silver, precious stones, wood, hay, stubble. The fire tests the quality of every man's works, and some will be vessels of honor, and others will be vessels of dishonor. Those whose works are faulty material, wood, hay or stubble will be in danger of Kingdom exclusion. They will hear the words; "depart from Me you workers of iniquity for I never knew you." Christians can have the door to enter the Kingdom age shut on them. As Christ has warned, "You shall not enter the Kingdom of Heaven."

What is the price of living a carnal Christian life now, only to suffer the loss of the 1000-year rule of Jesus Christ called the Kingdom of Heaven in the future? It is apparent only the qualified sons of God are given the inheritance, and the right to rule and reign with Jesus Christ. Requires those saints who qualify to be raised in the first resurrection. For blessed and holy is he who has part in the first resurrection.

Revelation 20:4-7

4 And I saw thrones, and they sat upon them, and judgment was given unto them: and I saw the souls of them that were beheaded for the witness of Jesus, and for the word of God, and which had not worshipped the beast, neither his image, neither had received his mark upon their foreheads, or in their hands; and they lived and reigned with Christ a thousand years.

5 But the rest of the dead lived not again until the thousand years were finished. This is the first resurrection.

6 Blessed and holy is he that hath part in the first resurrection: on such the second death hath no power, but they shall be priests of God and of Christ, and shall reign with him a thousand years.

7 And when the thousand years are expired, Satan shall be loosed out of his prison,

What Is the Inheritance Promised To Christ's Disciples

Chapter 6
Warnings of Kingdom Exclusion
Do All Christians Inherit the Kingdom of Heaven

I want to share with you one of the most challenging passages of Scripture for modern day Christians. In the 3rd chapter of Hebrews, the failure of Israel to enter their Promised Land is being discussed. The warning given to saints about Israel's failure comes when Gods people tempted the Lord ten times with their sin hardening their hearts in unbelief. When they came to the Promised Land which God said He would give them as an inheritance, they refused to enter. After which, Israel continued to tempt, and prove the Lord for forty years until their bodies fell in the wilderness outside what God had promised, their land of inheritance. Wherefore God was grieved with that generation, saying of them; "they do always error in their hearts, and have not known My ways."

One of the big issues overlooked by the modern Church is Gods oath of exclusion. You might remember when Israel refused to enter into the Promised land, the result of rebellion, and hard heartedness, God made an oath they would never enter; "I sware in My wrath, they shall not enter into My rest." So, one generation died because God would not give them a second chance. Instead they fell dead in the wilderness outside of the Promised Land. You might ask, how does this relate to Christians today?

The next part of the passage then warns Christians of their forfeiture and failure. "Take heed brethren, lest there be in any of you an evil heart of unbelief, in departing from the living God" (Hebrews 3:12)
What is the problem with this warning and why would so many modern Christians refuse to heed it?

1) It warns Christians of an evil heart of unbelief
2) It warns Christians they too can be hardened like Israel through the deceitfulness of sin

3) It makes for a "condition" upon Kingdom entrance based upon its fulfillment; "if we hold fast"
4) Christians are warned of failing to enter the rest of God, just like Israel failed
5) The rest of God is called the Kingdom, and it's entrance into the promised Kingdom at the end of this age identified as, "Partakers of Christ."
6) These passages warn Christians of their potential failure to enter the coming Kingdom age. Just like Israel did in failing to enter their inheritance at the end of their journey.
7) The reason they could not enter is their life of sin and unbelief after being brought out of slavery by the Blood of the Lamb. Ten times they tempted God in the wilderness leading to Gods promised oath of exclusion, His oath they would never enter.
8) So that generation died outside of Gods promised inheritance.

The warning is many Christians like sinful Israel will harden their hearts in sin, and at the Judgment Seat of Christ, God will refuse them entrance into the promised rest of the Millennial Kingdom. Just like Jesus warned His disciples, "Not everyone one who says Lord, Lord will enter the Kingdom of heaven, but they which do the will of My Father which is in Heaven."
(Matthew 7:21)

Now may Christians who can prophesy, who can work miracles, and who can cast out evil spirits be rejected by God at the Judgment Seat? Will Jesus Christ say to many Charismatics depart from Me you workers of iniquity? (Matthew 7:22).

Why don t modern Christians like the Judgment passages? Because they warn us who are born again of the consequences of a life of sin and unbelief. Many Christians only want to hear how well it will be because the Cross has saved them. However, these passages are warning about the walk of faith, and the results at the end of the journey. Simply put some Christians will be denied the right to enter the Kingdom based upon lives of unfaithfulness after being born again. God warns of loss of Kingdom age rewards, the denial by Jesus Christ at the Judgment. "Depart from Me", is Christs oath of exclusion saying you call Me Lord but I do not recognize you for Kingdom entrance. Your life of sin has excluded you; I do not recognize you for the Kingdom Age entrance you are shut out.

For an inheritance is given at the end of the journey, not the beginning. The Kingdom of heaven in Scriptures is always promised by inheritance. That's why Scriptures warn Christians in sin; "You shall not inherit the Kingdom of Heaven."

Hebrews 3:6-19

6 But Christ as a son over his own house; whose house are we, if we hold fast the confidence and the rejoicing of the hope firm unto the end.

7 Wherefore (as the Holy Ghost saith, To day if ye will hear his voice,

8 Harden not your hearts, as in the provocation, in the day of temptation in the wilderness:

9 When your fathers tempted me, proved me, and saw my works forty years.

10 Wherefore I was grieved with that generation, and said, They do alway err in their heart; and they have not known my ways.

11 So I sware in my wrath, They shall not enter into my rest.)

12 Take heed, brethren, lest there be in any of you an evil heart of unbelief, in departing from the living God.

13 But exhort one another daily, while it is called To day; lest any of you be hardened through the deceitfulness of sin.

14 For we are made partakers of Christ, if we hold the beginning of our confidence stedfast unto the end; 15 While it is said, To day if ye will hear his voice, harden not your hearts, as in the provocation.

16 For some, when they had heard, did provoke: howbeit not all that came out of Egypt by Moses.

17 But with whom was he grieved forty years? was it not with them that had sinned, whose carcases fell in the wilderness?

18 And to whom sware he that they should not enter into his rest, but to them that believed not?

19 So we see that they could not enter in because of unbelief.

Christians With an Evil Heart of Unbelief

Is there a passage in the Bible which identifies Christians after being born again can have an evil heart? This might be surprising in modern day theology where Christians are downplaying sin, but yes, the Bible says Christians can be hardened into an evil heart by sin.
Hebrews 3:12-13
12 Take heed, brethren, lest there be in any of you an evil heart of unbelief, in departing from the living God.
13 But exhort one another daily, while it is called To day; lest any of you be hardened through the deceitfulness of sin.

Let's look at the facts: 1) Christians sin, and can sin to the point where their heart has become hard and calloused against God. 2) Christians should "exhort one any daily" against being hardened by sin, before we stand in Judgment. 3) Sin is the problem before we are saved, and sin is still a viable temptation after we are saved.

What is the cost of Christians in sin? They will not be partakers with Jesus Christ in ruling in the Kingdom age. Just like Israel failed to enter their Promised Land tempting the Lord 10 times, before God promised by "oath" that generation would not enter Gods promised (rest), their land of inheritance.

Let's look at the facts: 1) Christians with hardened hearts of sin are compared to those of Israel who "did not enter the promised land." 2) Entering the next age our promised land, "the rest which remains," which Christians are "exhorted to labor, and not sin" is based upon conditions. 3) You partake of Christ, "if" we remain steadfast in our walk with the Lord. 4) To partake with Christ in this case is not the "free gift of salvation," instead it's the "works of faith," required for the right to rule with Jesus Christ an the end of this age. 5) This is why Jesus Christ says; Not everyone who says to Me Lord, Lord shall enter the Kingdom of Heaven. 6) Rejection by Jesus Christ of Christians at the Judgment are called "workers of iniquity," they failed in their service after coming into saving faith. 7) Like unfaithful Israel they are shut out from their promised inheritance. The rest at the end of this age. 8) Therefore, there remains a rest for the people of God, let us "labor" lest any fail to "enter into that rest," shut out from entering the Kingdom age. (Labor = works of reward).

Hebrews 4:11
11 Let us labour therefore to enter into that rest, lest any man fall after the same example of unbelief.

Hebrews 3:14-19

14 For we are made partakers of Christ, if we hold the beginning of our confidence stedfast unto the end;

15 While it is said, To day if ye will hear his voice, harden not your hearts, as in the provocation.

16 For some, when they had heard, did provoke: howbeit not all that came out of Egypt by Moses.

17 But with whom was he grieved forty years? was it not with them that had sinned, whose carcases fell in the wilderness?

18 And to whom sware he that they should not enter into his rest, but to them that believed not?

19 So we see that they could not enter in because of unbelief.

Characteristics for Entering the Kingdom of Heaven

"Blessed are the poor in spirit for theirs is the Kingdom of Heaven." Have you ever seen how the characteristics of the Sermon on the Mount are completely contrary from the ways of the world? For instead of the kings and conquers inheriting the earth, the meek, those who serve the Lord will be given the rights of ruling the earth.

Those who suffering now, experiencing loss, picking up the Cross in self-denial are those who morn now. "Blessed are they which morn, for they shall be comforted." Those who suffer loss for the Lord now, will be the inheritors of the Kingdom when the Lord returns.

Those who thirst and hunger for righteousness, those who are pure in heart, those are holy, are called the children of God are qualified for the Kingdom. Identified at the Judgment Seat as those who qualified for the inheritance of Kingdom of heaven. Blessed and holy are they for they shall rule with Jesus Christ for 1000 years in the Kingdom age. Upon them the Second Death has no power, as they have been raised in the first resurrection, are immortal and can die no more.

What of suffering now, and having mercy for those who hurt you, who persecute you for your devotion to Jesus Christ? What of the grace of God which has given you the ability to suffer for His name? Are you merciful, a peacemaker, are you pure in heart; "rejoice and be exceedingly glad for great is your reward in heaven?" When men say all manner of evil against you and you take the buffeting with patience. Rejoice and be exceedingly glad for so did they persecute the prophets, "for yours is the Kingdom of heaven."

Now for the reality check. Are you suffering because you are living as a disciple of Jesus Christ? Do you realize righteous Godly living separates you from the present age? As a true disciple of Jesus Christ your life will not follow the tends of this present age. Your life will be a reproof, a correction, a light, and salt which exposes the corruption of sin. Your losses and persecution will be real, your pursuit of righteousness will separate you from the masses. You will be persecuted for righteousness sake. Not what you have done wrong instead of what you have done right in Godly living before the Lord. Yours is the coming future Kingdom, however, your loss now is very real now. Now let this hit home, the Sermon on the Mount demonstrates how true disciples of Jesus Christ live now to inherit the Kingdom at the Second Coming of Jesus Christ.

For I say unto you that unless "your righteousness" ....shall exceed the righteousness of the Scribes and Pharisees (religious pretenders), "you will in no way enter the Kingdom of Heaven." Many Christians will live like the world now and expect to "enter the Kingdom then." Will not happen, only the meek, only the pure of heart, only those who suffer for righteousness ... "shall see God."

Matthew 5:1-20
1 And seeing the multitudes, he went up into a mountain: and when he was set, his disciples came unto him:
2 And he opened his mouth, and taught them, saying,
3 Blessed are the poor in spirit: for theirs is the kingdom of heaven.
4 Blessed are they that mourn: for they shall be comforted.
5 Blessed are the meek: for they shall inherit the earth.
6 Blessed are they which do hunger and thirst after righteousness: for they shall be filled.
7 Blessed are the merciful: for they shall obtain mercy.

8 Blessed are the pure in heart: for they shall see God.

9 Blessed are the peacemakers: for they shall be called the children of God.

10 Blessed are they which are persecuted for righteousness' sake: for theirs is the kingdom of heaven.

11 Blessed are ye, when men shall revile you, and persecute you, and shall say all manner of evil against you falsely, for my sake.

12 Rejoice, and be exceeding glad: for great is your reward in heaven: for so persecuted they the prophets which were before you.

13 Ye are the salt of the earth: but if the salt have lost his savour, wherewith shall it be salted? it is thenceforth good for nothing, but to be cast out, and to be trodden under foot of men.

14 Ye are the light of the world. A city that is set on an hill cannot be hid.

15 Neither do men light a candle, and put it under a bushel, but on a candlestick; and it giveth light unto all that are in the house.

16 Let your light so shine before men, that they may see your good works, and glorify your Father which is in heaven.

17 Think not that I am come to destroy the law, or the prophets: I am not come to destroy, but to fulfil.

18 For verily I say unto you, Till heaven and earth pass, one jot or one tittle shall in no wise pass from the law, till all be fulfilled.

19 Whosoever therefore shall break one of these least commandments, and shall teach men so, he shall be

called the least in the kingdom of heaven: but whosoever shall do and teach them, the same shall be called great in the kingdom of heaven.
20 For I say unto you, That except your righteousness shall exceed the righteousness of the scribes and Pharisees, ye shall in no case enter into the kingdom of heaven.

Christians Who Walk After the Flesh Lose the Kingdom

I have stated the Kingdom of heaven is treated as a future event at the Second Coming of the Lord. Dozens of passages which show the timing of the Kingdom, and how Christians are warned of Kingdom forfeiture by being disqualified at the Judgment Seat of Christ. The apostle Paul clearly spells this out in his letter to the Church at Galatians, where he warns those who walk after the flesh; "shall not inherit the Kingdom of God." (Galatians 5:21)

Here are the facts, an inheritance is given when one generation passes their blessing to the next generation. So, the Kingdom of Heaven age is given as an inheritance to qualified Christians who live faithful devoted lives, as a reward, a right to rule and reign with Jesus Christ at the Second Coming. The fact is the Kingdom is only given to those who have earned the right. Those Christians who disqualify themselves from inheriting the Kingdom are doing so right now by not living right with God in this age. That's why the Kingdom is not entered upon now as its entrance is at the first resurrection where qualified Christians are raised into immortality to rule with Christ. Its only at the end of this age qualified saints will "inherit the Kingdom," which means "they do not yet have the Kingdom." Now popular theology wants to make a much ado about how great the Kingdom of Heaven is now, but the Scriptures prove the Kingdom is future, and can be lost by disqualification. Which makes "no Christian" in the Kingdom age now, neither has any Christian already inherited the Kingdom.

Now many things in the lives of modern Christians will cause them to forfeit their future inheritance and be rejected from the Kingdom age. Here is Paul's list; adultery, fornication, uncleanness (perversity), and lasciviousness (lust). (Galatians 5:19) Do we not see an extraordinary amount of those who proclaim faith in Christ living in sexual sin, and are in bondage to lust? Though modern culture excuses these sins under the banner of the love and forgiveness of God. The Lord Jesus Christ will judge everyman without partiality and shut the door to the Kingdom age to all Christians who refuse to confess their immoral lifestyles. Christians living in sexual immorality shall not inherit the Kingdom of heaven, and you are in no way in the Kingdom spiritually now.

Now what about putting other things before God? (Idolatry) What about disobedience and rebellion? What about anger, hate, bitterness, and unforgiveness? What about all the Christian factions, divisions, and fighting among other Christians? (Church wars) What about all the famous men who preach heresy and divide the Church making followers of their false doctrines? All these things which are normally going on in the Church world will disqualify from the Kingdom Age those practitioners. So, the great men who declare themselves apostles and prophets who have twisted and corrupted the Word of God, who say the Kingdom is now, are by false doctrines disqualifying themselves and won't even be "entering the real Kingdom."

What about all the Christians who are getting high on weed, getting drunk on alcohol, who have abortions, and who are jealous and divisive? Without genuine confession of sin leading to repentance these works of the flesh will disqualify. Christians in unconfessed sin will often speak of the unfailing love of God. Christians who are a homosexual, Christians who are immoral, and condemned by your sinful actions, but excused by culture. Some born again Christians yield to the flesh living like the world, and have no real interest in the Church, and are even offended at the Church. Other Christians in unconfessed sin are getting caught up into listening to those who will itch your ears, saying your sins are already forgiven even though you have not repented. Other teachers saying all judgment on Christians has already past, and only the love of God without judgement remains. The reason you listen to false doctrine and teachers; "you want to continue in your sins." You refuse to be confronted, and act like your being put out when your life is being called into an account.

Maybe you are a preacher teaching the doctrine of demons called Universal Salvation. Which teaches in the end all men will be saved out of Hell. You tell men in sin what they want to hear. If you exposed their sin and warned of eternal judgment, the true doctrines of Christ, you would lose your audience and popularity. Others exploit the Church for personal profit, speaking of angels, and of revival, but are in it for the money. You're an extortionist holding the Church captive by your seduction and lies. Revival is not in your heart, as you hypocritically hide your own sins and make for appearances around your life and ministry which are inflated. You have deceived the body of Christ about the true nature of your own relationship with Jesus Christ. However, you always want to "been seen," to make a platform, an audience, and profit. Your own hypocrisy condemns you, but you put on a show to hide your real condition.

Will these imposters who are loved for their religious performance be given the Kingdom age? Let's make this simple; "they have their reward now." What they will hear at the Judgment Seat of Christ, "depart from Me you workers of iniquity for I never knew you." The door to the Kingdom age is shut to all whose righteousness is hypocrisy, whose walk after coming into saving faith is after the flesh. Sadly, what is going on in typical modern Christianity by Christians walking after the flesh will at the Judgment Seat of Christ be disinherited from entering the Kingdom age. "Not everyone who says to Me Lord, Lord shall enter the Kingdom of heaven, but only those who do the will of My Father in Heaven." (Matthew 7:21)

Galatians 5:17-21
17 For the flesh lusteth against the Spirit, and the Spirit against the flesh: and these are contrary the one to the other: so that ye cannot do the things that ye would.
18 But if ye be led of the Spirit, ye are not under the law.
19 Now the works of the flesh are manifest, which are these; Adultery, fornication, uncleanness, lasciviousness,
20 Idolatry, witchcraft, hatred, variance, emulations, wrath, strife, seditions, heresies,
21 Envyings, murders, drunkenness, revellings, and such like: of the which I tell you before, as I have also told you in time past, that they which do such things shall not inherit the kingdom of God.

The Sabbath Rest
Conditional Promise Based Upon If

Have you ever seen in the Word of God promises which are based upon meeting certain conditions?

Is everything by the born-again experience given automatically simply based on the free gift of salvation? It cannot be, if a condition of performance is attached. The word "if," demonstrates a need for qualification. God promises you a reward, only "if" you meet these conditions.

Now in popular Christian theology almost all conditional promises of God have been overlooked and downplayed as already given based upon the completed works of Christ. So, when it comes to suffering loss based upon sin and lack of Godly living, Christians of today are hyped into believing there will be no future judgment or consequences of loss. However, the book of Hebrews demonstrates many conditional promises based upon Christians meeting certain qualifications.

Hebrews 3:6
6 But Christ as a son over his own house; whose house are we, if we hold fast the confidence and the rejoicing of the hope firm unto the end.

Hebrews 3:7
7 Wherefore (as the Holy Ghost saith, To day if ye will hear his voice,

Hebrews 3:14
14 For we are made partakers of Christ, if we hold the beginning of our confidence stedfast unto the end;

Let's look at this backdrop. God has written in Hebrews a comparison with the nation of Israel, and Christians who will be judged at the Second Coming. Hebrews records Israel failed to enter into the Promised Land based upon an evil heart of unbelief. The Scriptures then warn Christians of a similar problem of being rejected by God at the Judgment Seat of Christ. God warns Christians of having an evil heart of unbelief and will not "enter His rest at the end of the age."

So here are the facts based upon Christians meeting certain conditions in order to enter His rest at the end of the age. Not all Christians will qualify to be part of the household of God, who will be the King priest companions of Christ at the Second Coming. (Hebrews 3:6). Just like unfaithful Israel who could not enter in "their rest," many saints will not qualify for the coming Kingdom of Heaven age. The next age is based upon meeting certain conditions now for the right to enter in the future based upon meeting those conditions right now by righteous conduct and living.

Wherefore the Holy Ghost says, "today if you will hear His voice?" Based upon Gods Word, and obeying what God has said, many saints simply refuse to obey God. Now Israel rebelled against the Word of God tempting Him ten times in the wilderness. Finally, Israel rebelled refusing to enter the land of promise based upon an evil heart of unbelief. The Hebrew Scriptures then warn

Christians of a similar rebellion and failure to enter in the promised Kingdom at the end of this age.

The loss is one of the Kingdom, not the loss of salvation. God calls this rejection the "oath of exclusion," where He promises "they shall not enter My rest." Saved yes but rejected from the end of the age rest. Why will many saints fail to enter? The results of an evil heart of unbelief.
Therefore, their remains a rest for the people of God. Let us fear the failure of not entering that rest. "Let us therefore fear, lest, a promise being left us of entering into his rest, any of you should seem to come short of it." (Hebrews 4:1)

Hebrews 3:12-19
12 Take heed, brethren, lest there be in any of you an evil heart of unbelief, in departing from the living God.
13 But exhort one another daily, while it is called To day; lest any of you be hardened through the deceitfulness of sin.
14 For we are made partakers of Christ, if we hold the beginning of our confidence stedfast unto the end;
15 While it is said, To day if ye will hear his voice, harden not your hearts, as in the provocation.
16 For some, when they had heard, did provoke: howbeit not all that came out of Egypt by Moses.
17 But with whom was he grieved forty years? was it not with them that had sinned, whose carcases fell in the wilderness?

18 And to whom sware he that they should not enter into his rest, but to them that believed not?
19 So we see that they could not enter in because of unbelief.

The Oath of Exclusion

The New Testament Book of Hebrews is not often discussed in the modern-day Christianity. It is one of the New Testament books which clearly teaches on Christians being judged for the sin of apostasy. Some modern-day Christian teachers attempt to disown the Book of Hebrews saying it was only written for first century Jewish Christians. My response is to question wither or not Christians still commit the sin of apostasy today, and if God still judges His own people today? The answer is of course God still judges His own today, and the Church is exhibiting signs of a Great Falling Away as warned by Scriptures before the Second Coming of Jesus Christ. The Book of Hebrews then might be one of the most relevant passages of Scripture for today which warn Christians of future judgment and consequences of sin.

Did you know God spoke an "oath," to the nation of Israel when the turned their back on God, and refused to go into the Promised Land? If you remember they tempted the Lord ten times on the journey towards the promised land including worshiping the Golden Calf, and sexual immorality. In the wilderness they would murmur and complain against God, against His High Priest Arron, and against Moses the Christ like Prophet. When they saw the giants in the Promised Land they refused to enter, and then later changed their mind attempting to go in against God's warning. Do you know why the nation of Israel could not enter the promised Land? God had sworn an oath which excluded them from entering the Land, even though it was formerly promised by God as their inheritance.

"So I sware in my wrath, They shall not enter into my rest." (Hebrews 3:11)

God made an oath of exclusion where those who sinned against the Lord, whereby Gods oath kept them out of their inheritance their bodies falling in the wilderness. Did you know with them God was not pleased, and judged them by keeping them out of their Promised Land? God called their actions "evil," and provoked Him to anger, leading to His oath of exclusion as judgment against them. Did you know the same passages of Scriptures warns Christians of an "evil heart of unbelief in departing from the living God?" Here is a surprise to many modern-day Christians who have never heard a message warning against living in sin or turning your back on God. The Scriptures says beware "brethren," meaning those who are born again saints set apart by the Blood Sacrifice of Jesus Christ. The Bible warns Christians can have hard hearts against God hardened by the deceitfulness of sinful practices.

Can a Christian then be shut out from entering their Promised Land? The whole Book of Hebrews is a warning about Christians who will be excluded from "Gods rest at the end of this age." Meaning when the Lord Jesus Christ comes to set up the Kingdom of Heaven on earth, some Christians will not be allowed to enter. The Book of Hebrews is based upon conditional obedience after coming into saving faith, so the condition of "if," is placed in the promises. "For we are made partakers of Christ, "if" we hold the beginning of our confidence steadfast unto the end" (Hebrews 3:14) Can you see a future "partaking of Christ," by the condition of "if" you are faithful now with the Lord in this life. If not, you will be shut out from the "future rest of the millennial kingdom." Just like unfaithful Israel who could not enter because God had judged their sin and made an oath to shut them out.

"So, we see they could not enter because of unbelief." (Hebrews 3:19) Therefore a promise of rest from all our enemies remains at the Second Coming of Jesus Christ. The right to rule and reign with Jesus Christ in the Kingdom of Heaven age. Some Christians will not enter that rest being disqualified by not running the race of faith with patient endurance to obtain the right of being crowned. Many Christians will simply sell their birth right like Esau for the temporary pleasures of sin, and "shall not inherit the Kingdom of Heaven." Therefore, there remains a rest for the people of God; "Let us therefore fear, lest, a promise being left us of entering into his rest, any of you should seem to come short of it." (Hebrews 4:1)

Hebrews 4:1-3
1 Let us therefore fear, lest, a promise being left us of entering into his rest, any of you should seem to come short of it.
2 For unto us was the gospel preached, as well as unto them: but the word preached did not profit them, not being mixed with faith in them that heard it.
3 For we which have believed do enter into rest, as he said, As I have sworn in my wrath, if they shall enter into my rest: although the works were finished from the foundation of the world.

Hebrews 3:7-19
7 Wherefore as the Holy Ghost saith, To day if ye will hear his voice,
8 Harden not your hearts, as in the provocation, in the day of temptation in the wilderness:
9 When your fathers tempted me, proved me, and saw my works forty years.
10 Wherefore I was grieved with that generation, and said, They do always err in their heart; and they have not known my ways.
11 So I sware in my wrath, They shall not enter into my rest.

12 Take heed, brethren, lest there be in any of you an evil heart of unbelief, in departing from the living God.
13 But exhort one another daily, while it is called To day; lest any of you be hardened through the deceitfulness of sin.
14 For we are made partakers of Christ, if we hold the beginning of our confidence stedfast unto the end;
15 While it is said, To day if ye will hear his voice, harden not your hearts, as in the provocation.
16 For some, when they had heard, did provoke: howbeit not all that came out of Egypt by Moses.
17 But with whom was he grieved forty years? was it not with them that had sinned, whose carcases fell in the wilderness?
18 And to whom sware he that they should not enter into his rest, but to them that believed not?
19 So we see that they could not enter in because of unbelief.

Esau An Example of An Apostate Christian

By its very nature apostasy can only be committed by a person after first coming into saving faith, then denying the faith. The sin of apostasy can only be committed by born again Christians. This might be confusing to some who always teach the Lord keeps those He saves. However, the sin of apostasy is committed willfully against the Spirit of Grace.

Hebrews 10:29
Of how much sorer punishment, suppose ye, shall he be thought worthy, who hath trodden underfoot the Son of God, and hath counted the blood of the covenant, wherewith he was sanctified, an unholy thing, and hath done despite unto the Spirit of grace?

Notice what conditions are involved in committing the sin of apostasy. You trample underfoot the Son of God, when you openly deny Christ after being born again. An apostate Christian makes a willful decision to count the Blood of Jesus Christ wherein he has been forgiven and given eternal life of no value. All this betrayal of the Lord is done against the Holy Spirit who has given the saints grace for every situation in life.

Now Esau is set forth in the Book of Hebrews as a man who despised the inheritance, the right of Gods covenantal blessing, and sold his birth right for the "carnal pleasures" of sin for a season. Esau was the first-born son the legal heir to his father's kingdom, but sold his birth right making little of the future inheritance. When the time of the transfer of the kingdom came Esau was rejected though he sought it with tears. The right of the first born was given to Jacob who highly valued his father's inheritance. Jacob wrestled with both God and man for the right of the first-born son.

Now many modern-day Christians have wrongly assumed you can be a friend of the world, and still be a friend with God. Instead, the world has gained their affections and desires, and in a thousand ways over time you have sold out your devotion to Jesus Christ. A million times over you compromise with the world until the value of Christ is made nothing. Like Esau you have sold out your rights to a future kingdom rule, "you shall not inherit the kingdom of heaven."

What does this mean, were they never saved in the first place? Absolutely not, they are blood washed born again sons who never went through the process of discipline and maturation. They lived for sin, and maybe the sin of the grosser kind, as Esau was a fornicator. They are sons by birth, but illegitimate sons who never submitted to the correction and discipline of their Father. Their loss is at the Judgment Seat of Christ where they will be disqualified and shall not inherit the Kingdom of Heaven.

Does this mean they lose their salvation? The answer, once a Son always a Son by birth. They lose the right of the first-born Son the right of inheritance the right to the Father business and kingdom. They lose the right of being a King Priest in the next age where they would have ruled with Christ in the Millennial Kingdom. For Jesus Christ said, not everyone who says to Me Lord, Lord shall enter the Kingdom of Heaven, but only they who do the will of My Father. Their sonship is retained, but like Esau they are "disinherited from the Fathers kingdom. "Apostate Christians are disinherited

Christians who sold their birth right for things of this world. Having turned their backs on the Lord going back into the world.

At the Judgment Seat of Christ Apostate Christians fall into to the hands of a living God where vengeance is executed by God against his own sons. In this case vengeance is a form of rejection and discipline, not an abandonment of sons into Hell. Instead a disqualification, a losing of the crown, the loss of the prize of the high calling. As the apostle Paul warmed Christians who practice the works of the flesh, "you shall not inherit the Kingdom of God." (Galatians 5:21)

For we must all appear before the Judgment Seat of Christ to give an account for things done in the body. Things done both good and bad. Therefore knowing the terror of the Lord we persuade men…

Hebrew 10:26-36
26 For if we sin willfully after that we have received the knowledge of the truth, there remaineth no more sacrifice for sins,
27 But a certain fearful looking for of judgment and fiery indignation, which shall devour the adversaries.
28 He that despised Moses' law died without mercy under two or three witnesses:
29 Of how much sorer punishment, suppose ye, shall he be thought worthy, who hath trodden under foot the Son of God, and hath counted the blood of the

covenant, wherewith he was sanctified, an unholy thing, and hath done despite unto the Spirit of grace?

30 For we know him that hath said, Vengeance belongeth unto me, I will recompense, saith the Lord. And again, The Lord shall judge his people.

31 It is a fearful thing to fall into the hands of the living God.

32 But call to remembrance the former days, in which, after ye were illuminated, ye endured a great fight of afflictions;

33 Partly, whilst ye were made a gazingstock both by reproaches and afflictions; and partly, whilst ye became companions of them that were so used.

34 For ye had compassion of me in my bonds, and took joyfully the spoiling of your goods, knowing in yourselves that ye have in heaven a better and an enduring substance.

35 Cast not away therefore your confidence, which hath great recompence of reward.

36 For ye have need of patience, that, after ye have done the will of God, ye might receive the promise.

Without Holiness No Man Shall See God

Hebrews 12:14
14 Follow peace with all men, and holiness, without which no man shall see the Lord:

This Scripture is very troubling as it is written to Christians in the context of accepting or rejecting Gods discipline. Those saints who reject the discipline of the Lord are considered illegitimate sons. Can a Christian be born again, and still be rejected by God based on unholy living? The answer is yes, but the debate usually runs along the lines of losing your salvation or not. So, the not seeing God would be the loss of eternal life to some. However, the context seems to be a son given birth right by being the first born of the family but refusing the fathers training for the family inheritance. In this case it would be the forfeiture of the right of the first-born son.

To prove the point, the sentence is followed by the life of Esau. Who is the first born of Isaac but sold his birth right to his brother Jacob for a bowl of lintels? The contrast being Esau despised his birthright by making light of the father's family Inheritance. While Jacob wrestled with God and man to have the rights of the first born. The Scriptures demonstrate a child born of the father can lose the right of the first-born son by unholy living but is still considered part of the family. Esau did this very thing, living an immoral life considered the birth right of Gods inheritance a light thing. Esau was a fornicator who followed the worlds immoral state, while Jacob considered the right of the first born what to live for.

The Scriptures says an immoral son who won't receive the fathers training and discipline will not see God. In this case not seeing God means Esau lost the right of inheritance and was disinherited from the fathers blessing. When it came time for the father to recognize the right of the first-born son, Esau was rejected disqualified by a life of unholy living. Even though Esau repented at the time of the blessing, Esau being in tears, the right of the first born was placed upon Jacob instead. "Will not see God," means rejected from the coming inheritance of God. Isn't this the same warning the apostle Paul gives Christians who are living unholy lives after being born again?

Paul warns born again Christians of losing the rights of the family inheritance by disqualification the result of unholy living. In this case the inheritance of the first-born sons is identified as the Kingdom of heaven. As you can see in the Book of Hebrews are warnings given to Christians not to have an evil heart of unbelief in departing from the Lord. The comparison is to sinful Israel who was delivered by the "Passover Blood of the Lamb," but failed to enter their Promised Land at the end of their journey. The reason their bodies fell in the wilderness outside of the promised inheritance, was the result of sin. This blood delivered children of God rebelled against Gods direction and correction. So, it is with many Christians who live after the flesh after being born again.

The saints who like sinful Israel will disqualify themselves from the right of the first-born son, and the future entrance into the kingdom of heaven at the end of the age. That is why Jesus Christ also warned of failure to enter the Kingdom age with saints who fail in obedience. The kingdom age is the reward for all the saints who lived separated righteous holy lives during their lifetimes. Jacob did during his lifetime, Esau did not. Enter the Kingdom age through the straight and narrow way for few are they who will separate unto God receiving the full training and discipline which qualify them for the right of first-born sons. The right to rule and reign with Jesus Christ as immortal king priests in the next age.

Hebrews 12:14-17
14 Follow peace with all men, and holiness, without which no man shall see the Lord:
15 Looking diligently lest any man fail of the grace of God; lest any root of bitterness springing up trouble you, and thereby many be defiled;
16 Lest there be any fornicator, or profane person, as Esau, who for one morsel of meat sold his birthright.
17 For ye know how that afterward, when he would have inherited the blessing, he was rejected: for he found no place of repentance, though he sought it carefully with tears.

Warn the Rich Man of Kingdom Exclusion

Why would Jesus Christ warn His disciples about the corrupting influences of mammon? Why would Jesus Christ tell His disciples with food, clothing, and shelter be content? Do modern Christians realize the life of faith requires our pilgrimage walking towards the Second Coming of Jesus Christ? As this present evil age is not our home. What do the seeking of riches represent in opposition to the Christian faith? Do not the worlds riches represent the pull upon a person's life demanding their time, loyalty, and affection? Jesus Christ warns chasing the worlds riches will require despising the Lordship of Jesus Christ. You cannot serve God and mammon. So why is the modern American Church always attempting to market its wealth? Why are famous personalities inside the Charismatic Movement entitled to think they deserve millions of dollars? Men who have multimillion-dollar ministries, and even say God told them to seek to buy million-dollar jets and buildings?

The reason is simple, they do seek wealth, and even use the Church for their own personal profit. Inside of the wealthy Laodicean Church is a belief God's blessing is personal wealth. However, the teachings of Scripture warn the rich, and Jesus Christ warned how the rich man would have difficulty entering the coming Kingdom of Heaven. Why does a rich Christian have a problem with God? Jesus Christ asked the rich young ruler to sell all his wealth, take all the money and give it to the poor with no personal profit. Then from the place of complete dependence on Jesus Christ with no guarantee of wealth, pick up the Cross, and serve the Lord seeking to make new disciples. A life completely given without any of the worlds wealth and success living just by the basics, food, clothing, and shelter.

The rich man went away sad, unwilling to do what the Lord had required of Him. The reason, the rich man valued the worlds treasure, and could not give it to God. The rich man could not see the value of laying up treasure in heaven, and not treasure on earth. The rich man had a lot to lose by sacrificing all, where the poor man has nothing to lose, and can easily follow the command to sell all to follow the Lord.

What of the warning spoken by Jesus Christ, it will be easier for a camel to enter the eye of the needle than for a rich man to enter the Kingdom of heaven? Once again, the answer is simple. Those who follow riches now have their rewards, their riches and fame, and manmade glory. You cannot seek first the coming Kingdom age and serve the mammon of the world. Instead you will devout your life, your time, your affections, to seeking and making worldly wealth. Your rewards are now, whatever treasure you can accumulate now. However, for those who will sell all now to serve the Lord, giving up lands, and homes, and personal wealth and riches, God will reward in the coming Kingdom Age. Only those who have sold out all to follow Jesus Christ will qualify at the Judgment Seat of Christ for Kingdom age rewards. Even as the apostle Peter said, Lord we have forsaken all, and followed you, what shall we have, therefore? (Matthew 19:27)

Here is Christs answer; 28 And Jesus said unto them, Verily I say unto you, That ye which have followed me, in the regeneration when the Son of man shall sit in the throne of his glory, ye also shall sit upon twelve thrones, judging the twelve tribes of Israel. 29 And everyone that hath forsaken houses, or brethren, or sisters, or father, or mother, or wife, or children, or lands, for my name's sake, shall receive a hundredfold, and shall inherit everlasting life.
30 But many that are first shall be last; and the last shall be first. (Matthew 19:28-30)

Is it not obvious in order to gain kingdom age rewards you must sacrifice all now in order to qualify? A poor man has less of the worlds riches to lose in order to pay the full price for kingdom age rewards. God warns the rich to lay up a good foundation for the time to come. Christians are being tempted to live for the world's goods now. Instead of living by faith laying treasure in heaven, thereby obtaining the Lords riches in the Kingdom age. As Jesus Christ warned you cannot have both. The seduction has come into the modern Church you can serve both God and mammon; however, you see how money is making all their decisions. Some of the multimillionaire high profile Christians boast how they need to acquire multi million dollars jets in order not to fly commercial airlines with the demonized. Funny how the original apostles said gold and silver and personal riches they had none, but never bargained with the Lord before picking up the Cross and follow Him to their own deaths.

Peter and the rest of the apostles will enter the Kingdom age upon thrones qualified by their sacrifices in this age to rule and reign with Jesus Christ. Those who are high minded and won't serve the Lord by sacrificing their demands for riches, can ride in the multi-million dollar jets, and live in their multi-million-dollar mansions. For they have their rewards now. I warn the rich, the American Church leadership, the cost of the Kingdom is to sell all now to be rewarded then. Spending your wealth on building your name, your multi-million dollar ministries is your reward. The poor and meek of the earth will enter the Kingdom as Kings and Priests in the age to come, and you will be denied the right of rewards. You love your riches, that is your reward. You will go away with great sadness at the Judgment Seat of Christ. For you are guilty of putting wealth before the Lord and making a profit from the Church.

Chapter 7
Kingdom Parables
Reveal the Time of Kingdom of Heaven

When Jesus Christ went up to Jerusalem many who knew He was the Messiah, expected Jesus to take the Throne and deliver Israel from Roman conquest. Many did identify Jesus Christ as the Son of David, the legal heir to the Throne of David. When Jesus Christ announced the Kingdom of Heaven was at hand, He was declaring the fact the Messiah the delivery of Israel, the Son of David was now on the scene. The nation of Israel did not balk at the announcement of the restoration of the Kingdom to Israel, instead wrestled over Jesus Christ being the Son of David, the Messiah, the legal heir to the Throne.

As Jesus Christ was journeying towards Jerusalem many of His disciples thought the time of the Kingdom had come. James and John wanted to be positioned right next to Jesus, on his right hand and on His left once Jesus Christ was seated upon His throne. His disciples would also fight over who would be the greatest in the Kingdom. However, Jesus Christ set forth parables which gave clarification of the time of the Kingdom. Jesus Christ taught the Kingdom would not be now, instead first the Cross, and a long departure away. Only then at the Second Coming would come the Kingdom age.

The parable of the Pounds was given for this very reason, for those who thought the Kingdom would immediately appear. (Luke 19:11) Instead Jesus Christ taught would go away into a far country to obtain the Kingdom. Then after a long absence would return after receiving the Kingdom. Right now, Jesus Christ is seated in heavenly places at the right hand of the Father, who will release Jesus Christ back to the earth for the

Kingdom age. Until then the servants of the Lord must follow the command to occupy in faithfulness until the Second Coming.

For the saints to faithfully serve the Lord, He has given us talents and pounds which translates into how we live our lives while the Lord is away. When the Lord has after a long while having received the Kingdom comes back (Luke 19:15), the saints must then give an account on how they utilized their talents or pounds. The first servant has taken one pound and increased it to ten pounds, the second servant has increased one into five pounds. The Lord of those servants was quite pleased giving them "authority to rule over cities in the Kingdom age." (Luke 19:16-19) These men are obviously Christian servants who followed the Lord during their lifetimes, even though the Lord was delayed a long time in heaven. Now upon the Lords Second Coming bringing the Kingdom of heaven with Him, these servants are qualified to rule with Jesus Christ in the Kingdom age. However, the third servant bothers all Christians. Jesus Christ calls this servant "a wicked and unprofitable servant." The reason was the third servant would not expend his life in trade and development while the Lord was away. The Lord judged this Christian at the Second Coming a wicked and unprofitable Servant, has the pound taken from Him, and no mention of any kind of reward is given. Is this wicked servant a Christian born again and judged at the Second Coming? A Christian who suffered loss, and even punishment which most Christians are uncomfortable to admit.

Those enemies of the Lord, like the Sheep and Goats Parable are in danger at the Second Coming. Some even are Christians who will not follow Jesus Christ in this age and will suffer loss at the Judgment Seat of Christ. This is the reason why the Scriptures warn unless your righteousness exceeds the righteousness of the Scribes and Pharisees you will in no way enter the Kingdom of Heaven. Only those who have qualified in their lifetimes through faithful lives of service will be able to inherit the Kingdom at the end of this age.

Luke 19:11-28

11 And as they heard these things, he added and spake a parable, because he was nigh to Jerusalem, and because they thought that the kingdom of God should immediately appear.

12 He said therefore, A certain nobleman went into a far country to receive for himself a kingdom, and to return.

13 And he called his ten servants, and delivered them ten pounds, and said unto them, Occupy till I come.

14 But his citizens hated him, and sent a message after him, saying, We will not have this man to reign over us.

15 And it came to pass, that when he was returned, having received the kingdom, then he commanded these servants to be called unto him, to whom he had given the money, that he might know how much every man had gained by trading.

16 Then came the first, saying, Lord, thy pound hath gained ten pounds.17 And he said unto him, Well, thou good servant: because thou hast been faithful in a very little, have thou authority over ten cities.

18 And the second came, saying, Lord, thy pound hath gained five pounds.

19 And he said likewise to him, Be thou also over five cities.

20 And another came, saying, Lord, behold, here is thy pound, which I have kept laid up in a napkin:

21 For I feared thee, because thou art an austere man: thou takest up that thou layedst not down, and reapest that thou didst not sow.

22 And he saith unto him, Out of thine own mouth will I judge thee, thou wicked servant. Thou knewest that I was an austere man, taking up that I laid not down, and reaping that I did not sow:

23 Wherefore then gavest not thou my money into the bank, that at my coming I might have required mine own with usury?

24 And he said unto them that stood by, Take from him the pound, and give it to him that hath ten pounds.

25 (And they said unto him, Lord, he hath ten pounds.)

26 For I say unto you, That unto every one which hath shall be given; and from him that hath not, even that he hath shall be taken away from him.

27 But those mine enemies, which would not that I should reign over them, bring hither, and slay them before me.

28 And when he had thus spoken, he went before, ascending up to Jerusalem.

The Parable of Pounds demonstrates how Jesus Christ gave an equal amount to His ten servants, expected them to trade their pounds while away in His absence. When Jesus Christ returned (Second Coming), He had received the Kingdom, and wanted to know what each servant had gained by trading. For Jesus would judge each servant according to their works, the amount gained during His absence. The first servant had taken the single pound and by trading had gained 10 pounds. Jesus Christ responded by judging His servant as a good and faithful servant taking what little he had to serve the Lord. Notice the reward the servant was given "great responsibility in the Kingdom Age," he was given rule over 10 cities. The servant was obviously a Christian who faithfully served the Lord before the Second Coming of the Lord, and the first resurrection. As the servant was judged as faithful by the Lord at His coming, He was given the right as a resurrected immortal saint to rule with Christ in the Kingdom age.

The same is demonstrated by Jesus Christ for the second servant. He took his pound and traded making five pounds. The Lord judged him as faithful also and allowed him into the immortality of the first resurrection to rule with Jesus Christ in the Kingdom of Heaven being given five cities to rule. In the Parable of the Pounds It is very clear the Kingdom of Heaven did not appear in this age, Jesus Christ would return with the Kingdom, and judge the saints (Christians) for their works of service during His absence.

This has made many modern Christians uncomfortable as the emphasis in modern teaching has downplayed the necessity for good works after coming into saving faith. The other thing which modern Christians struggle is how they give an account when the Lord returns at the Judgement Seat of Christ. What is measured is works of service, not eternal life. The Cross has already judged our eternity, given us forgiveness of sin, and no man can "earn salvation by good works." So, the Judgment Seat does not judge our eternal salvation, instead works for reward or their loss.

Now comes the most alarming of Christians being judged at the Second Coming. The wicked servant who would not trade while the Lord was absent. The first mistake is for modern Christians to say this man was "never saved in the first place." However, there are plenty of Christians who once saved, do not devote their lives in service to Jesus Christ. Also, the Judgment Seat is the measure of things done by Christians not unbelievers as no unbelievers appear in judgment with Christians at the Judgement Seat. Unbelievers appear for Judgement at the Great White Throne and is about damnation into the Lake of Fire. The wicked servant is judged with the other servants who are declared good, and faithful. Christians must know the judgment upon a man or woman who won't serve the Lord after coming into saving faith. As the modern Church struggle with the Scriptures which teach this unfaithful Saint will suffer loss at the Judgment Seat of Christ.

The summary is this, the Kingdom of Heaven is future at the Second Coming. The Lord knew He would be absent from the earth for a long time. In His absence He expected His servants to give their lives in trading what the Lord has given them. When Christ returns in the future, the servants will be qualified by the Judgment Seat to see the measure of their rewards. The most faithful of the servants are given a greater reward in the Kingdom of Heaven. This is demonstrated by the authority and responsibility they will have to rule and reign with Jesus Christ on earth over Kingdom age cities. The good and faithful servants of Jesus Christ who gained in trade (good works), are judged by their good works and the increase created by their lives.

The wicked servant is also a Christian who is expected to serve during this age. However, buries his talent and won't lay down their life in service to Jesus Christ. The wicked servant is one who fails to obtain a reward at the Judgment Seat of Christ and is given no cities to rule during the Kingdom of Heaven age. This is one of those who the Lord warned not everyone who says to Me Lord, Lord shall enter the Kingdom of Heaven, but only he who does the will of My Father in Heaven. Instead of losing their salvation or were never saved in the first place these Christians lose the right to rule in the Kingdom age. Their will lose their reward, and will not inherit the Kingdom of Heaven, just like the Scriptures teach.

Parable of the Wheat and Tares

The Parable of the Wheat and Tares was given in a mixed multitude as a description using farming examples. Jesus was describing how this age would play out in spiritual warfare using examples of wheat being planted, and then weeds invading the harvest. The seeds of wheat represent the sons of the Kingdom, Christians who have come into saving faith. Where the tares also represent people, only this time the sowing is done by Satan, and are children of the wicked one.

The harvest is at the end of this present evil age when the wheat and tares are separated one from another. Until the time of harvest the wheat and tares grow side by side in the same field. The harvest is at the end of the age, which the Scriptures describe as the Tribulation. It is at the time of the end, what has been planted into the world comes into full maturation. The wheat being the Church of the redeemed has come to fruition at the end, as every tribe, tongues, kindred and nation will have Christian members born of the Holy Spirit. The Church in its full membership will have been finalized, and all who will be saved in this age are placed into the body of Christ.

The harvest of tares is also at the end of the age. It is a harvest of wickedness where the sons of the evil one has also come of age. The Scriptures warn at the end of the age wickedness will have come into fullness, as it will be as in the Days of Noah. Mankind will have lost all fear of the Lord, and a spirit of lawlessness will fill the whole earth. In the end the sons of the wicked one will worship Satan, and the Antichrist taking the Mark of the Beast as worshipers. All who take the Mark of the Beast are separated at the Second Coming of the Lord and cast into the Lake of Fire. This is the fiery furnace which the Lord describes where the tares are bundled together in the end time harvest and are then burnt.

The angels of the Lord are the harvesters in the Parable, which also demonstrates their activity in final judgement as seen in the Book of Revelation. Notice both a harvest of righteousness and wickedness come into fruition at the end of the age. The Kingdom of Heaven as represented by the Sons of the Kingdom in this age will always experience mixture. As we move towards the Second Coming wickedness will abound. The Bible also describes the end days as the time of Lot in Sodom, which demonstrates how the whole earth will be filled with sexual perversity and immorality.

Looking for an end time harvest without mixture is simply out of the question. The philosophy the Church can produce a Christian Utopia or cleanse the seven of culture making for Christian cities or nations before the Second Coming is sheer fantasy. The sons of the wicked one will come of full age the harvest of wicked, immoral, and lawlessness will abound on earth before the Second Coming. It is impossible to place the government of God on earth, as the Kingdom of Heaven in this age. It is not until the final judgments of the Book of Revelation have been demonstrated the sons of the evil one is separated by God's angels and cast into the fiery furnace.

"Then shall the righteous shine forth as the sun in the kingdom of their Father. Who hath ears to hear, let him hear." (Mathew 13:43) The timing of the establishment of the Kingdom of Gods rule on earth is after the judgment of the wheat and tares. The separation of the tares did not happen with the first coming of Jesus Christ, instead only created the Sons of the Kingdom. The age in which the sons shall shine forth as the sun is not until the wheat is separated from the tares. It is at that time the sons of God appear as newborn calves skipping out of their stalls (resurrection), and tread under their feet the ashes of the wicked. For the Son of God will have arisen with healing in His Wings.

Kingdom Parables demonstrate the mysteries of the Kingdom bringing clarity as to when the Kingdom age will arrive on earth. Until then the wheat and tares will grow together in this age coming into fruition at the end of the age. Which is the time of Harvest the final judgments of God, and the establishment of the Kingdom of Heaven on earth. Until that time the Church age is full of mixture.

Matthew 13:24-30
24 Another parable put he forth unto them, saying, The kingdom of heaven is likened unto a man which sowed good seed in his field:
25 But while men slept, his enemy came and sowed tares among the wheat, and went his way.
26 But when the blade was sprung up, and brought forth fruit, then appeared the tares also.
27 So the servants of the householder came and said unto him, Sir, didst not thou sow good seed in thy field? from whence then hath it tares?
28 He said unto them, An enemy hath done this. The servants said unto him, Wilt thou then that we go and gather them up?
29 But he said, Nay; lest while ye gather up the tares, ye root up also the wheat with them.
30 Let both grow together until the harvest: and in the time of harvest I will say to the reapers, Gather ye together first the tares, and bind them in bundles to burn them: but gather the wheat into my barn.

Matthew 13:36-43
36 Then Jesus sent the multitude away, and went into the house: and his disciples came unto him, saying, Declare unto us the parable of the tares of the field.

37 He answered and said unto them, He that soweth the good seed is the Son of man;

38 The field is the world; the good seed are the children of the kingdom; but the tares are the children of the wicked one;

39 The enemy that sowed them is the devil; the harvest is the end of the world; and the reapers are the angels.

40 As therefore the tares are gathered and burned in the fire; so shall it be in the end of this world.

41 The Son of man shall send forth his angels, and they shall gather out of his kingdom all things that offend, and them which do iniquity;

42 And shall cast them into a furnace of fire: there shall be wailing and gnashing of teeth.

43 Then shall the righteous shine forth as the sun in the kingdom of their Father. Who hath ears to hear, let him hear.

Leaven in the Kingdom

When reading the Scriptures, it's possible to inject your own opinions or philosophy into the passage. In the Charismatic Movement, passages which speak of the Kingdom are often spun around to fit with a Triumphant Church mentality. The concept of a defeated Church, or a Church falling into error, or falling into apostasy is not permitted. Why does this "optimistic philosophy" push the agenda of so many in the Signs and Wonders Charismatic Movement?

The philosophy of the Church taking over the world and Christianizing the 7 Pillars of culture cannot be accomplished by the Charismatic Church and is losing the battle. So, any Scriptures which demonstrates sin, and human failure in the Church is then manipulated to fit with Charismatic Kingdom Now optimism. To excuse any conditions which exposes the deception of the Charismatic worldwide Church take over philosophies.

Let me provide you with an example. Leaven in the Bible is never treated as something good or beneficial. Leaven is often referred to as sin, which when uncorrected will spread through the whole loaf, or Church body corrupting the entire body of believers. Paul uses this example to Corinthian Christians who were not reproving and correcting sexual sin in their midst.

1 Corinthians 5:6-8
6 Your glorying is not good. Know ye not that a little leaven leaveneth the whole lump? 7 Purge out therefore the old leaven, that ye may be a new lump, as ye are unleavened. For even Christ our passover is sacrificed for us: 8 Therefore let us keep the feast, not with old leaven, neither with the leaven of malice and wickedness; but with the unleavened bread of sincerity and truth.

Now Jesus Christ also spoke of leaven, however Jesus used leaven as an example when referring to false doctrine. Did you get that? The corrupting influence of false teaching and false teachers is so great, its capacity is like leaven spreading its corruption throughout. What happens to Charismatics when they face the threat of false doctrines spreading throughout the whole Charismatic Movement? They have in the past either completely denied or ignored the issue or spin the Scriptures to say the "exact opposite" of what the Scriptures are warning.

For example when Jesus Christ teaches on the Parables of the Kingdom, Jesus warns of leaven spreading throughout.

Matthew 13:33 "Another parable spake he unto them; The kingdom of heaven is like unto leaven, which a woman took, and hid in three measures of meal, till the whole was leavened."

The Parables of the Kingdom all speak of corrupting influences in this age, like the Wheat and Tares Parable. What is noted in these Parables is mixture and corrupting influences. Now if I am a Charismatic teacher of the worldwide Church takeover, I need to spin the Scriptures which speak of a polluted and contaminated Church. So, what will I spin the Parable of Leaven to say? I will make leaven to be a good influence and say it's spreading throughout the Church is a good thing.

Here is an example of typical Kingdom Now optimism which is taught throughout the entire Kingdom Now Charismatic Movement:
"The leaven is the Kingdom of Heaven, and the Church spreads the Kingdom all over the world making the nations Christian, before Jesus Christ can return."

Do you see how Charismatic optimism creates "false doctrine," to bend and twist Scriptures which expose their beliefs as false? In no way is the Parable of the Leaven, about the Church spreading the Kingdom all over the world. Instead the Parable of Leaven warns of corrupting influences like sin, and false doctrines, which will contaminate the Church all the way to the Second Coming. The Parables of the Kingdom warns of mixture and corruption as demonstrated by the influences of leaven.

Let's get real, my optimistic denial does not give me the permission to alter the Scriptures to say something it has never said. The grave danger of this practice is seen in the Charismatic Passion Translation Bible where the philosophy of Kingdom Now is twisted into the Bible by adding or subtracting words. I shout out a clear warning, you are on the devils playground, and are guilty of spreading the leaven. The Word of God has exposed your deception and reproved your false beliefs, even if you don't agree. You fight God when you corrupt His Word by changing the Scriptures and rewriting them by adding or subtracting words to alter their meanings. God warns, you are under His curse.

Galatians 1:6-12
6 I marvel that ye are so soon removed from him that called you into the grace of Christ unto another gospel:
7 Which is not another; but there be some that trouble you, and would pervert the gospel of Christ.
8 But though we, or an angel from heaven, preach any other gospel unto you than that which we have preached unto you, let him be accursed.
9 As we said before, so say I now again, If any man preach any other gospel unto you than that ye have received, let him be accursed.
10 For do I now persuade men, or God? or do I seek to please men? for if I yet pleased men, I should not be the servant of Christ.
11 But I certify you, brethren, that the gospel which was preached of me is not after man.
12 For I neither received it of man, neither was I taught it, but by the revelation of Jesus Christ.

Harvest at Time of Kingdom

The parables given in Matthew chapter 13 give insights into the mysteries of the Kingdom. One thing main principle is obvious about the primary parable of the wheat and tares, this age is one of mixture. Have you noticed the closer we get to the Second Coming of Jesus

Christ, an open acceptance of perversity, sin and corruption is manifesting inside organized Christianity? Which confirms the message which the Wheat and Tares parable warns, both would grow side by side until the Second Coming of the Lord. Also as the day approaches both the wheat and tares would put on the head of ripened fruit indicating its ripened for harvest. In this case the tares which represent the sowing of Satan, is a growing and a more developed mature crop of corruption inside organized Christianity. Anyone who wants to open their eyes can see the new levels of acceptance of sin inside Christian organization. A moving towards apostasy which is a departure from the authority of Scriptures and Bible morality.

Now when the tares are fully ripened it's time for harvest, as harvest is at the end of the age. Jesus Christ said it would be as in the days of Noah when violence filled the whole earth and the thought of man was continually evil. Also, as in the days of Lot and Sodom, when wholesale homosexual lifestyles were openly celebrated and practiced. In both these cases the Lord was about to judge the sin and perversion, but the peoples of the earth were unaware the wrath of God was about to destroy them.

Matthew 13:37-43

37 He answered and said unto them, He that soweth the good seed is the Son of man;

38 The field is the world; the good seed are the children of the kingdom; but the tares are the children of the wicked one;

39 The enemy that sowed them is the devil; the harvest is the end of the world; and the reapers are the angels.

40 As therefore the tares are gathered and burned in the fire; so shall it be in the end of this world.

41 The Son of man shall send forth his angels, and they shall gather out of his kingdom all things that offend, and them which do iniquity;

42 And shall cast them into a furnace of fire: there shall be wailing and gnashing of teeth.

43 Then shall the righteous shine forth as the sun in the kingdom of their Father. Who hath ears to hear, let him hear.

Notice how at the time of the Kingdom at the end of this age, all the impure mixture is separated out. The harvesting angels gather the tares, the evil sowing, separating them from the ripened harvest of wheat, the sons of the Kingdom. All things which would offend making for impure mixture are separated at the time of the Kingdom. Until the time of the Kingdom both the wheat and tares can grow up together side by side. In the Church age mixture is its characteristic, in the Kingdom age separation, and purity is its characteristic.

Parable of the Drag Net

Matthew 13:47-50
47 Again, the kingdom of heaven is like unto a net, that was cast into the sea, and gathered of every kind:
48 Which, when it was full, they drew to shore, and sat down, and gathered the good into vessels, but cast the bad away.
49 So shall it be at the end of the world: the angels shall come forth, and sever the wicked from among the just,
50 And shall cast them into the furnace of fire: there shall be wailing and gnashing of teeth.

Notice once again in the Drag Net Parable the principle of the Kingdom being established by separating the good from the evil. So, shall it be at the "end of this age," when the angels of God shall come forth and sever the wicked from among the just. The kingdom is defined by separation at the end of this age, the judgments of the just and unjust. The wicked are separated out and casted into the fiery furnace of Hell. The Scriptures are clear the harvest is at the end of this age, at the time of the harvest the garnering of the wheat is into heavenly places, and the wicked in the judicial fires of Hell. This completely confirms with the record of the Book of Revelation which describes in detail Gods harvesting angels of judgment. Dramatic proof the Kingdom is prepared at the end of the age, at the Second Coming, and by separating the wheat from the tares. A multitude of passages demonstrate a

Kingdom of heaven is the future at the Second Coming, and not Kingdom Now.

Revelation 14:14-20
14 And I looked, and behold a white cloud, and upon the cloud one sat like unto the Son of man, having on his head a golden crown, and in his hand a sharp sickle.
15 And another angel came out of the temple, crying with a loud voice to him that sat on the cloud, Thrust in thy sickle, and reap: for the time is come for thee to reap; for the harvest of the earth is ripe.
16 And he that sat on the cloud thrust in his sickle on the earth; and the earth was reaped.
17 And another angel came out of the temple which is in heaven, he also having a sharp sickle.
18 And another angel came out from the altar, which had power over fire; and cried with a loud cry to him that had the sharp sickle, saying, Thrust in thy sharp sickle, and gather the clusters of the vine of the earth; for her grapes are fully ripe.
19 And the angel thrust in his sickle into the earth, and gathered the vine of the earth, and cast it into the great winepress of the wrath of God.
20 And the winepress was trodden without the city, and blood came out of the winepress, even unto the horse bridles, by the space of a thousand and six hundred furlongs.

Parable of the Ten Virgins
Marriage Supper in Kingdom Age

With the teachings of Scripture one event which helps
describe the inauguration of the Kingdom is the
Marriage Supper of the Lamb. It is obvious the time of
presentation of the Bride of Christ is at the end of the
age. The Parable of the Ten Virgins demonstrate only
five are qualified to enter the Marriage Supper, while
the other five did not have enough oil. The reality of the
whole Church being the Bride of Christ is simply not
true. Only the Bride revealed at the end of the age is
qualified in Judgment, for the "Bride has made herself
ready."

The qualification for Marriage Supper entrance is the
"righteous acts of the saints," not the righteousness
which comes with the free gift of salvation. Instead, acts
of service after coming into saving faith. This matches
with other Parables which demonstrate works are
Judged, for rewards, or loss of rewards. Simply put to be
the Bride of Christ in the Kingdom age, Christians are
qualifying now by righteous acts, which is the clean
linen worn by the Bride of Christ. The Brides garment is
accomplished by what you have done in living a life of
devotion after coming into saving faith.

Revelation 19:7-9

7 Let us be glad and rejoice, and give honour to him: for the marriage of the Lamb is come, and his wife hath made herself ready.

8 And to her was granted that she should be arrayed in fine linen, clean and white: for the fine linen is the righteousness of saints.

9 And he saith unto me, Write, Blessed are they which are called unto the marriage supper of the Lamb. And he saith unto me, These are the true sayings of God.

Now a foreshadowing of the Marriage Supper is given by the Lord at the Last Supper before His crucifixion. Jesus Christ sat down with the twelve disciples and ate a covenantal meal with them. At that time Jesus Christ stated He would not eat this meal again until its inauguration in the Kingdom age. Which once again proves the Kingdom of heaven is future, at the Second Coming, and with the first resurrection. Dozens of passages demonstrate the Kingdom of Heaven is given as an inheritance rewarded to those Christians who qualify for it. Just like five virgins are shut out of the Marriage Supper, "I do not know you." Jesus Christ did not say they were workers of iniquity, or weren't saved, instead they were not qualified for the Marriage Supper entrance.

The Marriage Supper of the Lamb is one of the highest rewards given in the Kingdom age. Simply put not all Christians will be allowed that privilege honor, as in this lifetime they did not devote themselves to Jesus Christ.

Also, Jesus Christ will not eat the Marriage Supper until the advent of the Kingdom Age. These are sure proofs the Kingdom is not now, instead is the future coming Kingdom.

Luke 22:15-30
15 And he said unto them, With desire I have desired to eat this passover with you before I suffer:
16 For I say unto you, I will not any more eat thereof, until it be fulfilled in the kingdom of God.
17 And he took the cup, and gave thanks, and said, Take this, and divide it among yourselves:
18 For I say unto you, I will not drink of the fruit of the vine, until the kingdom of God shall come.
19 And he took bread, and gave thanks, and brake it, and gave unto them, saying, This is my body which is given for you: this do in remembrance of me.
20 Likewise also the cup after supper, saying, This cup is the new testament in my blood, which is shed for you.
21 But, behold, the hand of him that betrayeth me is with me on the table.
22 And truly the Son of man goeth, as it was determined: but woe unto that man by whom he is betrayed!
23 And they began to enquire among themselves, which of them it was that should do this thing.
24 And there was also a strife among them, which of them should be accounted the greatest.

25 And he said unto them, The kings of the Gentiles exercise lordship over them; and they that exercise authority upon them are called benefactors.
26 But ye shall not be so: but he that is greatest among you, let him be as the younger; and he that is chief, as he that doth serve.
27 For whether is greater, he that sitteth at meat, or he that serveth? is not he that sitteth at meat? but I am among you as he that serveth.
28 Ye are they which have continued with me in my temptations.
29 And I appoint unto you a kingdom, as my Father hath appointed unto me;
30 That ye may eat and drink at my table in my kingdom, and sit on thrones judging the twelve tribes of Israel.

Parable of the Mustard Seed

The Parable of the Mustard Seed demonstrates the perversion of growth which happens in this present evil age. Many who spin the Scriptures would spin this parable to mean the Kingdom of Heaven is spread all over the earth filling the world a mighty tree. However, the seed is the mustard seed which produces a small unassuming low-lying bush. A perversion of the mustard seed comes from a change of nature from a small bush growing into a mighty tree which houses the fowls of the air. Is this not the description of what has happen to organize Christianity when Constantine mixed Church and state creating a pagan perversion inside organized Christianity.

A super structure has emerged a perversion from original Christianity of the first two centuries. The paginated Christian Church became a mighty super structure called Catholicism filling the earth with doctrines of demons and Church traditions. This is the mighty tree which has emerged from the unassuming mustard seed, and the Lord never intended the Church to marry with the world. The fowls of the air which have found a home in its branches are the evil spirits behind the doctrines of demons taught by the Super Structure of Catholicism. Now the perversion of Protestantism can be added to the Super Structure.

Mathew 13:31-32

31 Another parable put he forth unto them, saying, The kingdom of heaven is like to a grain of mustard seed, which a man took, and sowed in his field:

32 Which indeed is the least of all seeds: but when it is grown, it is the greatest among herbs, and becometh a tree, so that the birds of the air come and lodge in the branches thereof.

Parable of Leaven

The Parable of the Sower, and the Parable of Mustard Seed have demonstrated corruptibility and mixture in this age in things related to the Kingdom of Heaven.

We have been shown the wheat and tares grow side by side in this age until the time of the harvest at the end of the age. We also have been shown the unnatural growth of the Mustard Seed into a superstructure which houses evil spirits in its branches. In the Parable of Leaven, the concepts of corruption are continued this time from inside. The concept of Leaven is its ability to transform the whole loaf. In this case Leaven is not treated as a good influence instead the power of corruption.

In Scriptures Leaven is related with two influences, one is sin, the other false doctrine and practices. In the Parable of Leaven, the woman takes leaven and mixes it with three measures of meal. Often in Scriptures the female is representative of the Church, so this likely is a demonstration of how the Church is corrupted by sin in its midst, and from false teachers and doctrines of demons. This is a challenge to all who think the Church is purified in this age. As the Scriptures warn of perilous times in the last days, and apostasy, the concept of a purified Bride in this age is false. When Jesus Christ comes, He will separate out from the Church, a Glorious Church, His Bride without spot or wrinkle. Until then the Church will be contaminated by sin, and mixture, with Wheat and Tares growing together. In fact, the Lord will come in a time when the Great Harlot Mystery Babylon will have joined herself to the Antichrist as the Great counterfeit Bride.

The woman can corrupt the entire loaf, which is how sin can spread through the Church. Here is an example of sexual sin not being corrected by the Church, and the apostle Paul's warning of how it can spread like leaven throughout the whole Church. "Your glorying is not good. Know ye not that a little leaven leavened the whole lump?" (1 Corinthians 5:6) You can see how sexual sin today is corrupting the Church. Church leaders of today have compromised the faith and are sympathetic with same sex marriage, and gay rights. Even many have supported abortion upon demand calling it Gods choice. The Church near the end of this age is leavened by immoral practices of Christians living together outside of marriage, and the lack of confrontational preaching and excommunication.

Jesus Christ compared man made traditions and false doctrine to the influences of leaven when exposing the hypocrisy of the Pharisees.
"How is it that ye do not understand that I spake it not to you concerning bread, that ye should beware of the leaven of the Pharisees and of the Sadducees? Then understood they how that he bade them not beware of the leaven of bread, but of the doctrine of the Pharisees and of the Sadducees." (Matthew 16:11-12)

The concepts of a glorious end time Church which sanctifies the seven pillars of culture is a doctrine of demons. The Church at the end is contaminated with the leaven of doctrines of demons and threatens the

Church with apostasy. The very philosophy of a Church which transforms the world making for Christian nations and cities is the spreading of leaven. Instead the Bible warns in the last days many shall depart from the faith, giving heed to seducing spirits (teachers), and doctrines of demons. (1 Timothy 4:1) Perilous times mark the Church of the last days as evil men and imposters wax worse, and worse deceiving and being deceived. The conditions of a leavened Church are present today, and Christians are in danger of growing cold in their love as a lawless spirit is being celebrated throughout the world.

Will Christians return to the Word of God and the doctrines of Christ as their final authority? Sadly, the answer is no. As the apostle Paul warns a time will come, as is even now when Christians will turn from sound doctrine to the leaven of manmade philosophy, and will only want to have their ears itched by the false doctrines from Church leaders. They will lust after perverted doctrines and heap to themselves teachers who will tell them the fairy tales they want to hear. Are the 3 measures of meal which Jesus Christ predicted would become fully leavened by sin and perverse doctrine, now completely present in our day?

1 Corinthians 5:1-8
1 It is reported commonly that there is fornication among you, and such fornication as is not so much as

named among the Gentiles, that one should have his father's wife.

2 And ye are puffed up, and have not rather mourned, that he that hath done this deed might be taken away from among you.

3 For I verily, as absent in body, but present in spirit, have judged already, as though I were present, concerning him that hath so done this deed,

4 In the name of our Lord Jesus Christ, when ye are gathered together, and my spirit, with the power of our Lord Jesus Christ,

5 To deliver such an one unto Satan for the destruction of the flesh, that the spirit may be saved in the day of the Lord Jesus.

6 Your glorying is not good. Know ye not that a little leaven leaveneth the whole lump?

7 Purge out therefore the old leaven, that ye may be a new lump, as ye are unleavened. For even Christ our passover is sacrificed for us:

8 Therefore let us keep the feast, not with old leaven, neither with the leaven of malice and wickedness; but with the unleavened bread of sincerity and truth.

Matthew 13:33-35

33 Another parable spake he unto them; The kingdom of heaven is like unto leaven, which a woman took, and hid in three measures of meal, till the whole was leavened.

34 All these things spake Jesus unto the multitude in parables; and without a parable spake he not unto them:

35 That it might be fulfilled which was spoken by the prophet, saying, I will open my mouth in parables; I will utter things which have been kept secret from the foundation of the world.

Matthew 16:11-12

11 How is it that ye do not understand that I spake it not to you concerning bread, that ye should beware of the leaven of the Pharisees and of the Sadducees?

12 Then understood they how that he bade them not beware of the leaven of bread, but of the doctrine of the Pharisees and of the Sadducees.

2 Timothy 4:1-4

1 I charge thee therefore before God, and the Lord Jesus Christ, who shall judge the quick and the dead at his appearing and his kingdom;

2 Preach the word; be instant in season, out of season; reprove, rebuke, exhort with all longsuffering and doctrine.

3 For the time will come when they will not endure sound doctrine; but after their own lusts shall they heap to themselves teachers, having itching ears;

4 And they shall turn away their ears from the truth, and shall be turned unto fables.

The Parable of Buried Treasure

The Parables of Matthew 13 are about the conditions which will exist in the Church age before the establishment of the Kingdom of Heaven on earth at the Second Coming of the Lord. As the Kingdom of Heaven was founded before the formation of the Church, its presence transcends this present evil age. As the Kingdom was first given to Israel in its worldwide dominance with King David and Solomon, it has been lost ever since. With the first coming of Jesus Christ, the Son of David announced the Kingdom of Heaven was at hand, but Israel rejected its Messiah. The establishment the Kingdom has then been delayed until the Second Coming of Jesus Christ when He will that time bring the Kingdom of Heaven with Him, and the millennial reign of Christ on earth will begin then.

Mathew 25:34
34 Then shall the King say unto them on his right hand, Come, ye blessed of my Father, inherit the kingdom prepared for you from the foundation of the world:

In Scriptures we are given a picture of the Kingdom, during the reign of King David. Jesus Christ was announced to be the prophesied Son of David, who would restore the Kingdom to Israel. Jesus Christ announced the Kingdom was at hand, but Israel rejected her King. The Kingdom was then delayed until the Second Coming of Jesus Christ. A huge error is made by the Kingdom Now teachers when attempting to make the Church the Kingdom of Heaven on earth and make for millennial conditions in this age. The Parable of the Buried Treasure demonstrates how the Kingdom is discovered then buried, it is the treasure of the Parable.

Matthew 13:44
44 Again, the kingdom of heaven is like unto treasure hid in a field; the which when a man hath found, he hideth, and for joy thereof goeth and selleth all that he hath, and buyeth that field.

After the fall of Israel into Babylonian capacity the Kingdom in essence was buried. The Old Testament Prophets spoke of its restoration to Israel, by King David's Son. God had promised to King David he would never lack a Son to sit on the Throne of David. When Jesus Christ announced the Kingdom of Heaven was at hand, He was properly identified by some as the Son of David, the legal heir to the Throne. As Israel rejected their King, the Kingdom was delayed, and the Gentiles are also offered the capacity to enter the Kingdom of Heaven by faith in Christ. The process of Jesus Christ selling everything in order to obtain the Kingdom is a description of the Cross and Resurrection. Jesus Christ by His sinless perfection, Cross, and Resurrection has been declared the first-born Son the legal heir to His Fathers Throne. The right of the first born is given Him, that's why the Scriptures identify Jesus Christ as our Melchizedek our King and Priest.

Jesus Christ said the Kingdom of Heaven would be delayed and men would long to see His day. For almost two thousand years, the Church age, the Kingdom of Heaven has been recurred, as the rule of Christ on earth is not seen among the Governments of the nations. However, the beastly nature of the world's Kingdoms is transformed when Jesus Christ returns as the King of Kings and the Lord of Lords. It is at the time of the first resurrection, men like Abraham, Isaac, and Jacob are raised from the dead into immortality to rule and reign with Jesus Christ from the New Jerusalem on earth. When the Lord returns the Kingdoms of this present evil age become the kingdom of our Lord and His Christ.

Until then the Kingdom of Heaven is like hid treasure waiting for the Lords return. When Christ returns the Kingdom will be restored as promised and prophesied by the prophets of Old. To put the Kingdom in this age without the resurrection of the dead, and the immortal saints ruling with Christ is to twist the Scriptures. The Kingdom of Heaven restores Israel as the head of the nations, to twist the Scriptures to say otherwise is to deny the facts clearly stated. The treasure which the Scriptures call an inheritance is given to men and woman who qualify to rule and reign with Jesus Christ. The crown and throne are not given in this age, instead the saints must run the race of faith, so they may obtain an imperishable crown. Right now, we have a lot of Christians running around acting like little kings, but they have no cloths no crown. Pretend kings who will stand naked before God at the Judgment Seat of Christ being disqualified from Kingdom of Heaven entrance.

Revelation 11:15-19
15 And the seventh angel sounded; and there were great voices in heaven, saying, The kingdoms of this world are become the kingdoms of our Lord, and of his Christ; and he shall reign for ever and ever.
16 And the four and twenty elders, which sat before God on their seats, fell upon their faces, and worshipped God,
17 Saying, We give thee thanks, O Lord God Almighty, which art, and wast, and art to come; because thou hast taken to thee thy great power, and hast reigned.
18 And the nations were angry, and thy wrath is come, and the time of the dead, that they should be judged, and that thou shouldest give reward unto thy servants the prophets, and to the saints, and them that fear thy name, small and great; and shouldest destroy them which destroy the earth.
19 And the temple of God was opened in heaven, and there was seen in his temple the ark of his testament: and there were lightnings, and voices, and thunderings, and an earthquake, and great hail.

Chapter 8
The Kingdom and Judgment Seat of Christ

When the Scriptures are measured concerning the coming Kingdom of Heaven, the Judgment Seat of Christ is an important factor. In Scriptures salvation comes as a free gift of grace, however, the Kingdom is always connected with works of faith for reward. The simple way of revealing the difference is salvation comes without any human merit, while the Kingdom is based upon our "acts of righteousness" after coming into saving faith. Wherever you see Jesus Christ teaching on the Kingdom, works of righteousness are connected. That's why Jesus Christ said, unless "your righteousness" exceeds that of the Scribes and Pharisees you will in no wise enter the Kingdom of Heaven. (Matthew 5:20) Your righteousness is based upon works of faith, not the free gift of the Cross, and the righteousness which comes from God. Of course, in the Christian faith all things related to the Kingdom require the Grace of God to walk in them. So even in good works of faith, there must be a complete dependence on Jesus Christ.

Now the Scriptures demonstrate in Judgment, God measures every man according to their works. Notice in this passage the reward given by God is called an inheritance, and God gives to every man what they deserve according to "what they have done," for with God there is no respect of persons. He is an impartial judge. In other passages the Kingdom of Heaven is treated as an inheritance given to qualified saints at the end of the age.

Colossians 3:23-25
23 And whatsoever ye do, do it heartily, as to the Lord, and not unto men;
24 Knowing that of the Lord ye shall receive the reward of the inheritance: for ye serve the Lord Christ.
25 But he that doeth wrong shall receive for the wrong which he hath done: and there is no respect of persons.

Now the Judgment Seat is the time of measuring the works of all Christians. Each Christian will appear at their Tribunal to give an account for things done in their body, things done by both good and bad. How does the Judgment Seat test you, by Gods judicial fire? The fire will test the quality of every man's work to see what manner of material. If the Christians life has been one of self-serving, their materials will be defective, wood, hay, and stubble. The fire reveals the true nature of the persons works after coming to saving faith. The fire burns up the defective Christian works, revealing the defective material. These Christians will suffer great loss, but their salvation remains intact. What is tested are works of reward or their loss, not the works of the Cross which has bought their redemption. As the Cross has already judged the saints for eternal salvation. While defective materials is a life lived for self, the fire burns up all the self-centered works and there is no Kingdom Age rewards. As Jesus Christ warned His disciples; Not everyone who says to Me Lord, Lord shall enter the Kingdom of Heaven, but only those "who do the will of My Father in Heaven." (Matthew 7:21)

Now the words at the Judgment Seat which no Christian will want to hear; "depart from Me you workers of iniquity for I never knew you." This is a Christian who failed at the Judgment Seat of Christ. Their loss is failure to enter the Kingdom age; "shall not enter the Kingdom of heaven." Jesus Christ does not recognize them for Kingdom entrance and shuts the door of the Kingdom Inheritance; "you shall not inherit." (Matthew 7:21-23)

Do modern day Charismatics understand many who profess before God; I prophesied in your name, worked many mighty miracles in your name, and cast out evil spirits, will fail the Judgment Seat. Let me be frank, "multimillion-dollar ministries," who exploited the Church for their own personal profit, making their fortunes off the Church... will fail at the Judgment Seat. "They built their own little empires," and refused to pick up the Cross seeking first the Kingdom of heaven. Jesus Christ warned His disciples with food and clothing be content for it will be hard for a rich man to enter the Kingdom of heaven. Those who taken the things of God and used them for themselves calling it "the blessing of God," will be exposed for their hypocrisy at the Judgment Seat of Christ.

One more thing all these famous apostles in the Charismatic Movement who are constantly teaching heresy and drawing away men unto themselves are in danger of being disinherited from the Kingdom of heaven. Their riches and fame are their rewards now. For heresy will exclude them from the Kingdom age. (Galatians 5:20-21)

2 Corinthians 5:9-11
9 Wherefore we labour, that, whether present or absent, we may be accepted of him.
10 For we must all appear before the judgment seat of Christ; that everyone may receive the things done in his body, according to that he hath done, whether it be good or bad.
11 Knowing therefore the terror of the Lord, we persuade men; but we are made manifest unto God; and I trust also are made manifest in your consciences.

1 Corinthians 3:10-15
10 According to the grace of God which is given unto me, as a wise master builder, I have laid the foundation, and another buildeth thereon. But let every man take heed how he buildeth thereupon.
11 For other foundation can no man lay than that is laid, which is Jesus Christ.
12 Now if any man build upon this foundation gold, silver, precious stones, wood, hay, stubble;

13 Every man's work shall be made manifest: for the day shall declare it, because it shall be revealed by fire; and the fire shall try every man's work of what sort it is.
14 If any man's work abide which he hath built thereupon, he shall receive a reward.
15 If any man's work shall be burned, he shall suffer loss: but he himself shall be saved; yet so as by fire.

Should Christians Fear the Judgment Seat

One of the strangest things happening inside modern organized Christianity is the absence of any kind of the fear of the Lord. With all manner of Charismatics saying they are going into heaven, and holding conversations with Jesus Christ, I have never heard one profess an absolute "fear of being in God's presence." Even the most intimate of apostles, the apostle John fell as a dead man in the presence of Jesus Christ after seeing Christ in a vision after the Resurrection. Instead of fear of the Lord, Charismatics speak of God with such "familiarity," as to call Him, daddy God, or Poppa, or Bridal romantic association. Where has the fear of the Lord gone inside the modern Charismatic Church?
One place has a very peculiar warning for Christians, it's the Judgment Seat of Christ. The apostle Paul warns every Christian must appear at the Judgment Seat of Christ when the Lord returns, to give an account for things done in their body. Not just the good things, but also the bad things will be exposed and judged with

impending consequences. Since only Christians appear at the Judgment Seat, you would think Paul would speak in an optimistic way to encourage the saints about their future judgement. However, after warning all Christians must appear before our Judge, Jesus Christ, Paul does not speak of mercy and grace. Instead Paul warns of "the terror of the Lord," which speaks of the difficulty the saints face when giving an future account for the life after coming to saving faith.

Why would Paul warn saved Christians of the terror of the Lord? Paul says because of the terror of the Lord, Christians need to be warned. Perhaps modern-day Christianity has neglected Scriptural passages which speak of judgment, rebuke, punishment and loss. In these passages the character and nature of Jesus Christ is one of an impartial judge. Several passages demonstrate judgment upon Christians to the severest level. For example, in the Book of Acts, reveals God judged Ananias and Sapphira unto death. Also, Paul's example of delivering over the immoral brother in Christ to Satan for the destruction of his flesh. In this case a Christian who is unwilling to repent of sexual immortality is being put under judgment, where Satan will be the instrument of destruction. So, God will judge, rebuke and chastise Christians even unto death.

Now the God of Ananias and Sapphira is also judge over all Christians at the Judgment Seat of Christ. The Lord will judge all men without impartiality and will give everyman their due at the Judgment Seat of Christ. Unfortunately, not every Christian will be receiving God's blessing and rewards. Some Christians who have lived Godless lives, burying their talents refusing to serve the Lord will be met with correction and rebuke. Some Christians will be called "wicked and unprofitable servants," and will be cast into outer darkness where there is weeping and gnashing of teeth.

Why is there the terror of the Lord? God as judge has made Hell to punish the soul of the unrighteous in flames of Hell Fire judgment. Also made the Lake of Fire, to raise the man whose name is not written in the Book of Life back into their bodies, and then placed into the Lake of Fire for eternal judgment. The same Lord will come out of heaven at the Last Trump to battle the nations of the earth in the Battle of Armageddon. God who made man in His image, is the Father of all, but will judge the earth with fire upon His return. Let's get this straight the Lord God who sends men into the Lake Fire for an eternity will not overlook the godlessness of Christians.

Why is the argument about Christian judgment always about once saved always saved, or loss of salvation? Should not the issue include the character and nature of God. For it is a fearful thing Christian to fall into the hands of the living God. And again, for those who sin willfully, a fearful looking to the future loss, the punishment, and the correction at the Judgment Seat of Christ.

Hebrews 10:26-31

26 For if we sin willfully after that we have received the knowledge of the truth, there remaineth no more sacrifice for sins,

27 But a certain fearful looking for of judgment and fiery indignation, which shall devour the adversaries.

28 He that despised Moses' law died without mercy under two or three witnesses:

29 Of how much sorer punishment, suppose ye, shall he be thought worthy, who hath trodden under foot the Son of God, and hath counted the blood of the covenant, wherewith he was sanctified, an unholy thing, and hath done despite unto the Spirit of grace?

30 For we know him that hath said, Vengeance belongeth unto me, I will recompense, saith the Lord. And again, The Lord shall judge his people.

31 It is a fearful thing to fall into the hands of the living God.

2 Corinthians 5:9-11

9 Wherefore we labour, that, whether present or absent, we may be accepted of him.

10 For we must all appear before the judgment seat of Christ; that every one may receive the things done in his body, according to that he hath done, whether it be good or bad.

11 Knowing therefore the terror of the Lord, we persuade men; but we are made manifest unto God; and I trust also are made manifest in your consciences.

Can the Blood of Jesus Save You from the Judgment
Seat

Probably one of the most neglected areas of teaching in
modern day Christianity concerns the Judgment Seat of
Christ. So neglected is the doctrine that many Christians
believe the "grace of God" has covered all their
behavior(s) to have no further case for concern. The
simple thought is "saved by the blood" and forgiven
having eternal life and heaven after death. However,
the scriptures reveal the Blood of Jesus Christ cannot
save you from the coming day of accountability. Even
though a Christian has been given eternal life all saints
must go through "a judgment" at the end of the age
giving account for things done after coming to saving
faith.

How little the Church is warned of the difficulties to be
found at the Judgment Seat of Christ. For at the
Judgment Seat of Christ is the measurement of "works
of faith" which will allow the saint to qualify for ruling
with Christ in the next age or be disinherited from the
age. The difficulty of qualification is very serious as Paul
warns the entire Church of the possibility of
"disinheriting." How important is our lives and manner
of living after coming into saving faith?

What does it mean to be disinherited at the end of the
age? Simply put the Christian appears at the Judgment
Seat of Christ and has their life works tested by fire.

All works which do not measure up by sinful Godless living are burned up in the fire. The saint who loses all in the fire will be disinherited from the Kingdom of heaven. The loss of the Kingdom means the saint has not qualified for the first resurrection, not the loss of their eternal life. Instead are shut out, "depart from Me you workers of iniquity for I never knew you." (Matthew 7:23)

At the Judgment Seat carnal living by the saints is equal to selling out your birthright for the pleasures of sin. Like Esau who was the first-born son and should have inherited his Father's blessing Esau was rejected from that right by godless living. The right of the first-born son then was passed unto Jacob who had highly valued the right of the first-born son. Only those Christians who wholly followed the Lord in this life will be crowned for the Kingdom age as the inheritors of the "Church of the First Born." All others who do not qualify at the Judgment Seat will be disinherited although their eternal life remains intact. They come through the fires of God having lost the Kingdom but have still retained the salvation of eternal life. Saints coming through the fire having all their defective works burned up, and only the foundation being saved which maintains eternal life. Coming through the fire losing everything smelling like smoke but their life is not burned up.

1 Corinthians 3:11-15
11 For other foundation can no man lay than that is laid, which is Jesus Christ.

12 Now if any man build upon this foundation gold, silver, precious stones, wood, hay, stubble;
13 Every man's work shall be made manifest: for the day shall declare it, because it shall be revealed by fire; and the fire shall try every man's work of what sort it is.
14 If any man's work abide which he hath built thereupon, he shall receive a reward.
15 If any man's work shall be burned, he shall suffer loss: but he himself shall be saved; yet so as by fire.

Why at the Judgment Seat Your Issues Are Not Overlooked

I have seen a few recent articles from a famous Charismatics magazine which attempted to say why this famous apostle is a good guy. Another article spoke of a woman who had been in Christian television for decades as a Godly woman. While many issues of character, and sin have been exposed in their lives. A common practice has emerged in the modern Church, a practice for Christians to overlook the bad, and speak only of the good. In this way the image of the person is preserved in the eyes of others even though the facts and truth of how they have really lived would bring shame and reproach. The modern Church often lacks the ability to bring correction, discipline, or even rebuke. The result is many actions which are ungodly, wicked, or evil are then swept under the carpet and hidden or not fully exposed. Christians might excuse these actions in terms of friendship, or to save face, or to preserve money or ministry. However, God is not a respecter of persons, God will not be mocked for whatsoever a man sows he will reap.

As you know the Christian life is wrought with many trails, tests, temptations, and sin. A man's reputation can be upheld by those around him even if his actions are sinful. On the other hand, God will judge a Christian without partiality according to what they have done. That's why in the Bible, the sins, and failures of Gods leaders are exposed and not glossed over. Even the most celebrated of God leaders are exposed in the sins, and hypocrisy. Afterward, we see how God chooses to rebuke, discipline, or correct their actions. The Bible is clear, Gods judgement is alive and active. Christ's word of judgement is sharper than any two-edged sword which exposes our motives. The thoughts and intents of the heart, as all things are naked and open in the sight of God nothing is hidden from Him. Therefore, every man will be without excuse as the motives and intent of the heart will be clearly revealed so everyman will be without excuse.

Now the final judgment of Christians is at the Second Coming of Jesus Christ, and at the Judgment Seat of Christ called the Bema in New Testament Greek. All Christians will stand before the Lord to give an account for things done in our body after coming into saving faith. Things we have done both good, and bad. The judicial fire of God will test the quality of every Christian one person at a time. If the fire burns up the material by which you lived your life you will suffer loss. Some Christians will come through the Bema fires smelling like smoke as everything they have done is burned up under the intense examination of Gods judgment. Your loss will be great, just like Esau who sold his birthright for a bowl of lentils, who later sought the inheritance with tears "was declared reprobate." Even the apostle Paul who suffered some much for the Lord warned of his loss, if he did not bring his body under subjection. Paul too, would have been declare reprobate if he failed in his consecration.

Why does the Scripture warm Christians of the terror of the Lord at the Bema judgment? The answer is simple, God will judge His people, and it is a fearful thing to fall into the hands of a living God. Modern Christianity has attempted to remove all judgment so nothing of consequences or responsibility remains. A false Gospel of which all are rewarded the same. A false Gospel which gives false comfort, and false peace. The fear of the Lord has been removed from Gods house and the saints have failed to consult with the Scriptures concerning their future. Many saints on that day will attempt to justify their lives before the Lord protesting how they have prophesied, worked miracles, and cast out evil spirits. However, the Lord will not be persuaded, He commands them to depart judging them workers of iniquity. Even today the Charismatic Church has many evil practices which go uncorrected.

Part of the issue is the fame and popularity of those leaders who are being exposed but have refused correction. It will be a sad day for famous leaders to be cast "outside the Kingdom," as they boasted for so long in bringing the Kingdom from heaven to earth. Their fantasy life will be exposed by the facts of judicial fire. Their false doctrines, and manmade glorification will burn up in smoke. In the end the glory they are receiving from man now is "their reward." As they exchanged the glory of man for the coming rewards of Gods glory.

2 Corinthians 5:9-16
9 Wherefore we labour, that, whether present or absent, we may be accepted of him.
10 For we must all appear before the judgment seat of Christ; that every one may receive the things done in his body, according to that he hath done, whether it be good or bad.
11 Knowing therefore the terror of the Lord, we persuade men; but we are made manifest unto God; and I trust also are made manifest in your consciences.
12 For we commend not ourselves again unto you, but give you occasion to glory on our behalf, that ye may have somewhat to answer them which glory in appearance, and not in heart.
13 For whether we be beside ourselves, it is to God: or whether we be sober, it is for your cause.
14 For the love of Christ constraineth us; because we thus judge, that if one died for all, then were all dead:

15 And that he died for all, that they which live should not henceforth live unto themselves, but unto him which died for them, and rose again.

16 Wherefore henceforth know we no man after the flesh: yea, though we have known Christ after the flesh, yet now henceforth know we him no more.

1 Corinthians 9:24-27

24 Know ye not that they which run in a race run all, but one receiveth the prize? So run, that ye may obtain.

25 And every man that striveth for the mastery is temperate in all things. Now they do it to obtain a corruptible crown; but we an incorruptible.

26 I therefore so run, not as uncertainly; so fight I, not as one that beateth the air:

27 But I keep under my body, and bring it into subjection: lest that by any means, when I have preached to others, I myself should be a castaway.

The Resurrection and The Kingdom

Have you seen in the Charismatic Church how many teachers declare the Kingdom of Heaven is now by the Church? However, the Scriptures tell us a different story as the Kingdom is identified with Abraham, Isaac and Jacob. It seems the Abrahamic Covenant promised by God to Abraham and his seed gave them the right of rule over the earth. Furthermore, in line with the same Covenantal promise, God gave promise to King David, there would never lack a Son of David to sit upon the

Throne of David for all eternity. The point being the right of Kingdom rule was promised by God to these Old Testament saints which obviously predates the formation of the New Testament Church.

Why is it the Charismatic Apostolic Movement refuses to see the future context of the Kingdom on earth? Is it not a belief God has divorced Himself from the nation of Israel, and the Church has inherited the promises given to Israel? This makes absolutely no sense as Old Testament prophets constantly affirm the eternal nature of Gods covenantal promise to restore Israel. So Abraham, Isaac, and Jacob, as well as King David, and the Prophets must be included in the Kingdom age. Jesus Christ confirms the coming Kingdom age, when Jesus Christ takes the Throne of David as the Son of David to rule the earth from the New Jerusalem, He would sit down with Abraham, Isaac and Jacob at the Marriage Supper of the Lamb. This would require these Old Testament saints would be raised from the dead.

In Scriptures we see the constant affirmation of the Kingdom of heaven being connected to the Resurrection of the righteous dead. So important is this absolute fact, God promised the twelve apostles who would die as martyrs would be raised into the Kingdom age and would sit on 12 thrones ruling and reigning with Jesus Christ from the New Jerusalem. Here is a fact, the Kingdom of Heaven is never separated from the resurrection of the righteous. When the Church declares itself the Kingdom of Heaven on earth it attempts to rule by Church government without immortality. The Bible clearly teaches the saints which rule in the Kingdom are immortal and are not subject to corrupted bodies anymore.

The Kingdom without the resurrection of Abraham, Isaac, and Jacob is simply not the Kingdom of heaven promised by God. Also, Jesus Christ warned the Kingdom would be by qualification, as He warned many Jews who thought they would attain to it simply by Jewish birth would be cast out. When the Rich man inquired what would be the cost to "inherit the Kingdom," Jesus Christ told him to go sell all his riches give all the money to the poor, and come follow Him as a poor lowly disciple. The Rich man went away sad for he had great riches. Jesus Christ then said it is hard for a rich man to enter the Kingdom of Heaven. It would be easier for a camel to go through the eye of a needle than for a rich man to enter the Kingdom of heaven. Why is this true? The worlds goods become a man's kingdom now, and wealthy men build their own kingdoms refusing to sell all to follow Jesus Christ for future Kingdom age rewards.

It's the same in the Charismatic Church today. Multi-millionaire apostles with huge platforms attempt to teach the Church the Kingdom is now. They want the Church to take over the world and are constantly holding religious conferences becoming wealthy by their false doctrine. They teach the Kingdom is of this world without Abraham, Isaac, Jacob, and the 12 apostles. They say the Church will Christianize the world by the Kingdom of heaven brought to earth by the Church. However, never has there been even one Christian city, or nation in almost 2000 years. These men are building a manmade religious organization and are not even close to making the Kingdom of Heaven on earth.

A man must go through the eye of the needle to enter the Kingdom. He must pass from death into life, and from corruption to incorruption. The Kingdom age saint rules with Jesus Christ in an immortal body. Must I state the obvious, no man has the power to make himself immortal. If you fail to partake in the first resurrection you fail to enter the Kingdom age.

Matthew 19:16-30
16 And, behold, one came and said unto him, Good Master, what good thing shall I do, that I may have eternal life?
17 And he said unto him, Why callest thou me good? there is none good but one, that is, God: but if thou wilt enter into life, keep the commandments.
18 He saith unto him, Which? Jesus said, Thou shalt do no murder, Thou shalt not commit adultery, Thou shalt not steal, Thou shalt not bear false witness,
19 Honour thy father and thy mother: and, Thou shalt love thy neighbour as thyself.
20 The young man saith unto him, All these things have I kept from my youth up: what lack I yet?

21 Jesus said unto him, If thou wilt be perfect, go and sell that thou hast, and give to the poor, and thou shalt have treasure in heaven: and come and follow me.

22 But when the young man heard that saying, he went away sorrowful: for he had great possessions.

23 Then said Jesus unto his disciples, Verily I say unto you, That a rich man shall hardly enter into the kingdom of heaven.

24 And again I say unto you, It is easier for a camel to go through the eye of a needle, than for a rich man to enter into the kingdom of God.

25 When his disciples heard it, they were exceedingly amazed, saying, Who then can be saved?

26 But Jesus beheld them, and said unto them, With men this is impossible; but with God all things are possible.

27 Then answered Peter and said unto him, Behold, we have forsaken all, and followed thee; what shall we have therefore?

28 And Jesus said unto them, Verily I say unto you, That ye which have followed me, in the regeneration when the Son of man shall sit in the throne of his glory, ye also shall sit upon twelve thrones, judging the twelve tribes of Israel.

29 And every one that hath forsaken houses, or brethren, or sisters, or father, or mother, or wife, or children, or lands, for my name's sake, shall receive an hundredfold, and shall inherit everlasting life.

30 But many that are first shall be last; and the last shall be first.

Chapter 9
Why the Christian Faith Must Include the Next Age

When Jesus Christ proclaimed the Kingdom of God, He was declaring the rule of God over the nations. However, in Scriptures the nations are portrayed as wild beasts which are predatory in nature and devour of Gods people. As a result, the Christian is a misfit, a sojourner on a journey towards the Promised Land at the end of this age. The Christian is called out from the nations and joined to God in a holy nation, a royal priesthood who should show forth the praises of Him. Who has called you out of darkness into His marvelous light? Now for centuries the saints have looked for the city whose builder and maker is God. Virtually all have seen this promise afar off, never seeing the New Jerusalem descend out of Heaven to begin the Kingdom age.

The cost of true Christian journey is to identify with Christ, while not loving the world nor the things of the world. Jesus Christ put the seeking of the Kingdom first which means in this age the fullness of God could never really come. In the next age the saints will be raised into immortality and become as the angels of heaven. However, Jesus Christ also warned His disciples not everyone who calls Him Lord, Lord will enter the Kingdom age. Putting the age to come as the Christian reward will prove a difficult assignment for many Christians especially those who are rich in this age.

Jesus Christ declared it will be easier for the camel to go through the Eye of the Needle than a rich man to lay down this worlds treasure.

So many boasts in their riches, and their worldly success and attainments not realizing they have compromised with the Lord. In truth their earthly treasure is their reward now. They like Esau have sold their future birthright for this world's pleasures. As they stand in Judgment at the Second Coming of the Lord, Christ will call them workers of iniquity, and refuse to recognize them for Kingdom age rule and reign. Like Esau, they will lose the rights of the first born, and instead see their brothers who wrestled with God and man for the inheritance be given God's blessing of the Kingdom age. Though they weep with tears of remorse as Gods judgment stands and will shut them out from the rights of the first-born sons.

When does the Scripture say the Sons of God will appear? At the first resurrection and at the Second Coming of Jesus Christ. These are the saints who appear in their immortal glory, and rule with Jesus Christ for one thousand years with a rod of iron. Many saints will choose not to go through the straight and narrow way in this life and will not inherit Kingdom age stature and rewards. Paul calls the first resurrection the prize of the high calling and was willing to count all things lost in order to qualify for it. So Christian what kind of cost are you paying? For the kingdom is the same price for all and will cost you everything in order to inherit. Hardly can a man stand to lose this world in order to gain the Kingdom age rewards. Many will protest, but the Lord will say; "depart from Me."

Romans 8:16-39
16 The Spirit itself beareth witness with our spirit, that we are the children of God:
17 And if children, then heirs; heirs of God, and joint-heirs with Christ; if so be that we suffer with him, that we may be also glorified together.
18 For I reckon that the sufferings of this present time are not worthy to be compared with the glory which shall be revealed in us.
19 For the earnest expectation of the creature waiteth for the manifestation of the sons of God.
20 For the creature was made subject to vanity, not willingly, but by reason of him who hath subjected the same in hope,
21 Because the creature itself also shall be delivered from the bondage of corruption into the glorious liberty of the children of God.
22 For we know that the whole creation groaneth and travaileth in pain together until now.
23 And not only they, but ourselves also, which have the first fruits of the Spirit, even we ourselves groan within ourselves, waiting for the adoption, to wit, the redemption of our body.

24 For we are saved by hope: but hope that is seen is not hope: for what a man seeth, why doth he yet hope for?

25 But if we hope for that we see not, then do we with patience wait for it.

26 Likewise the Spirit also helpeth our infirmities: for we know not what we should pray for as we ought: but the Spirit itself maketh intercession for us with groanings which cannot be uttered.

27 And he that searcheth the hearts knoweth what is the mind of the Spirit, because he maketh intercession for the saints according to the will of God.

28 And we know that all things work together for good to them that love God, to them who are the called according to his purpose.

29 For whom he did foreknow, he also did predestinate to be conformed to the image of his Son, that he might be the firstborn among many brethren.

30 Moreover whom he did predestinate, them he also called: and whom he called, them he also justified: and whom he justified, them he also glorified.

31 What shall we then say to these things? If God be for us, who can be against us?

32 He that spared not his own Son, but delivered him up for us all, how shall he not with him also freely give us all things?

33 Who shall lay any thing to the charge of God's elect? It is God that justifieth.

34 Who is he that condemneth? It is Christ that died, yea rather, that is risen again, who is even at the right hand of God, who also maketh intercession for us.
35 Who shall separate us from the love of Christ? shall tribulation, or distress, or persecution, or famine, or nakedness, or peril, or sword?
36 As it is written, For thy sake we are killed all the day long; we are accounted as sheep for the slaughter.
37 Nay, in all these things we are more than conquerors through him that loved us.
38 For I am persuaded, that neither death, nor life, nor angels, nor principalities, nor powers, nor things present, nor things to come,
39 Nor height, nor depth, nor any other creature, shall be able to separate us from the love of God, which is in Christ Jesus our Lord.

Understanding Christian Pilgrimage

Today the modern Church is teaching to unify with the world, to be seeker sensitive, and adopt practices like the world to bring more Christian influence. Is the message of the Scriptures? Save the world by transforming culture speaking their language and adopting their philosophy into the Church. Why is this confusing, as in modern Christianity looks more like the world's entertainment than what the 1st century Church experienced. Instead Christians were burned as human torches, faced gladiators, and lions as entertainment in Roman arenas. To die as a Christian martyr giving witness was a very real part of Christian testimony in the first century Church. Of course, in many portions in the world Christians are still being martyred, but in America or Western Europe that type of persecution is rare. In portions of the world where Christianity has suffered a great threat from its culture, the Church is growing at incredible rates. In places of the world where the Church is conforming to the world, the Church is going into decline, and often considered irrelevant.

I find with American Christians the concepts of Lordship, separation from the world, and Christian pilgrimage is not often embraced. The. Biblical concept of God calling His people out from the world separating unto to Him is a primary message of Scriptures. The concept of saints separated out from the world in a journey towards the Second Coming of Jesus Christ, is called the pilgrimage of the faith. One of the great dangers which Christians face is to "stop pilgrimage," and settle down with the world system. Christians who are not walking a separated life living like the rest of the world knows very little about being a disciple of Jesus Christ by picking up the Cross in self-denial. A disciple of Jesus Christ has given up his own will and follows the Jesus Christ as the "Lord of his life."

What is the danger of world system? All its influences are completely contrary to the Christian faith. You cannot love the world, and love God at the same time, which are in complete opposition one to another.

Look at this warning from the apostle John who connects the love of the world with those who do not know the love of God the Father.

1 John 2:15-17
15 Love not the world, neither the things that are in the world. If any man love the world, the love of the Father is not in him.
16 For all that is in the world, the lust of the flesh, and the lust of the eyes, and the pride of life, is not of the Father, but is of the world.
17 And the world passeth away, and the lust thereof: but he that doeth the will of God abideth for ever.

Notice how apostle John characterizes what the world really holds: 1) the lust of the flesh 2) lust of the eyes 3) pride of life. John does not treat the world as charming, aesthetic, or beautiful. Instead John warns Christians the world represents the "same type of temptations," Adam and Eve faced from Satan in the Garden of Eden. The world leads away from God and directly to the Kingdom of darkness and the Prince of the Power of the Air, Satan. John connects all which is in the world with the antichrist spirit, and with walking in darkness and sin. I have found worldly Christians are in comprise with God with those very things. The more the Church attempts to become like the world, to be not offensive, the more offense to God those Christians have become. They are careful not to offend the world, but they are in compromise with God. Christians may get more attention, praise, honor, rewards, and wealth by taking their talents and serving the world, but they are lukewarm with God.

Show me a Christian who is successful with the "world's goods," the worlds praise and honor, I will show you a Christian who is in compromise with God. For what fellowship has light with darkness, or the Temple of God with the Temple of idols? Today the Church thinks it's making great advancements as it brings the worlds entertainment inside household of the faith. Instead it just indication how far removed modern Christians are from their pilgrimage with God.

Let's make it simple. Tell the world they are dead in their sins, on the way to Hell in need of salvation by the only way, the Cross of Jesus Christ. The next thing you will know is they will "try to hang you on the Cross," in abject hatred of what you have proclaimed. If you doubt that just ask Jesus Christ what happened to Him every time, He exposed evil in the world!

The Narrow Way

Narrow is the way which leads to life, and few are they which find it. Are there any more certain words as these spoken by Jesus Christ? What is more common to a man than a self-centered, self-love, and self-preservation, way of life? The masses of Christians are being tempted to abandon their separation and refuse to walk in the straight and narrow way. The broadways is the world's way, it is the self-life. Many are the saints who are born again of the Spirit, but never enter the narrow way of picking up the Cross in self-denial. The most unnatural way of this life is to suffer the loss of all things, to count all things loss, and to value those things as dung. Picking up the Cross being crucified to the world and yourself life. Do we not see how repulsive, how offensive, how unnatural the crucified life really is?

The context of the passage which Jesus Christ declared the narrow way was the Sermon on the Mount. Is there anything more backwards a more turned upside down life than the Sermon on the Mount? Characteristics of which Jesus Christ described for His true disciples were to live? Love your enemies, bless them which curse you, pray for them which despitefully use you, do good to them which hate you. Do you not see, the Cross of the disciple must sacrifice the world's values? Especially the highest value of all "putting yourself first."

Now many Christians assume because they are born again, God is in the business of promoting their lives. Many simply have taken their lives which were before Christ, and now after coming into saving faith still have failed to surrender the self-life. Many Christians have just put a God label on their selfishness and call it God's blessing. This kind of Cross-less Christianity is dominating modern day pulpits and is the commercial and entertainment world of the Church.

This present evil age is in complete contradiction to the walk of faith. The Christian is a stranger and pilgrim on a journey towards the Second Coming, and the Kingdom of Heaven on Earth. The loss must be real in this time, you must redeem the time for the days are evil. The Scriptures inform us not to be surprised at the fiery trails which have come upon our life as if some strange this was happening to us. "But rejoice," for the outcome of suffering with Christ's sufferings is loss now, but when Christ is revealed in glory (Second Coming) you may glad with "exceeding joy."
Apostle Peter teaching about the walk of faith said the saints must suffer reproach for Christ. Peter teaches God's will for your life is to suffer for well doing. As the result God orders your environment will many personal crosses to train and discipline your walk for the next age. Many things which come along in our life cause us to suffer loss. To see the self-life crucified, if you don't have your eyes on the Lord personal loss and suffering can lead to offense at Christ.

Many are the offended in Christ, who have stopped walking in the straight and narrow way. They have thought the cost of their personal Cross to be too high a price. They have left off from the Lord to walk in the broad way of a self-centered love and have refused the Cross. The broad way is their course, in which they have their "reward now." Christian do you understand the narrow way is about the Christian journey, and the trials of our faith, which are God's way of ordering our environment of the Cross? Once you enter the straight gate coming into saving faith in Christ, the way of faith is to fellowship in the sufferings of Christ. The shame, the pain, the loss, the rejection, the aloneness is a very narrow way indeed.

However, as the apostle Paul has said the in the face of his enormous suffering; "this light affliction is bit for a moment is working in me an exceedingly eternal weight of glory." Paul had his eyes on the prize of the high calling in Christ, and knew the Cross was before the Throne. Anyone who refuses the Cross in this age will not be qualified for the next. In this way, many Christians will face their own demise following the crowds who refuse the fellowship of the Cross.

Matthew 7:13-14
13 Enter ye in at the strait gate: for wide is the gate, and broad is the way, that leadeth to destruction, and many there be which go in thereat:
14 Because strait is the gate, and narrow is the way, which leadeth unto life, and few there be that find it

1 Peter 4:12-19
12 Beloved, think it not strange concerning the fiery trial which is to try you, as though some strange thing happened unto you:
13 But rejoice, inasmuch as ye are partakers of Christ's sufferings; that, when his glory shall be revealed, ye may be glad also with exceeding joy.

14 If ye be reproached for the name of Christ, happy are ye; for the spirit of glory and of God resteth upon you: on their part he is evil spoken of, but on your part he is glorified.

15 But let none of you suffer as a murderer, or as a thief, or as an evildoer, or as a busybody in other men's matters.

16 Yet if any man suffer as a Christian, let him not be ashamed; but let him glorify God on this behalf.

17 For the time is come that judgment must begin at the house of God: and if it first begin at us, what shall the end be of them that obey not the gospel of God?

18 And if the righteous scarcely be saved, where shall the ungodly and the sinner appear?

19 Wherefore let them that suffer according to the will of God commit the keeping of their souls to him in well doing, as unto a faithful Creator.

1 John 2:12-29

12 I write unto you, little children, because your sins are forgiven you for his name's sake.

13 I write unto you, fathers, because ye have known him that is from the beginning. I write unto you, young men, because ye have overcome the wicked one. I write unto you, little children, because ye have known the Father.

14 I have written unto you, fathers, because ye have known him that is from the beginning. I have written unto you, young men, because ye are strong, and the

word of God abideth in you, and ye have overcome the wicked one.

15 Love not the world, neither the things that are in the world. If any man love the world, the love of the Father is not in him.

16 For all that is in the world, the lust of the flesh, and the lust of the eyes, and the pride of life, is not of the Father, but is of the world.

17 And the world passeth away, and the lust thereof: but he that doeth the will of God abideth for ever.

18 Little children, it is the last time: and as ye have heard that antichrist shall come, even now are there many antichrists; whereby we know that it is the last time.

19 They went out from us, but they were not of us; for if they had been of us, they would no doubt have continued with us: but they went out, that they might be made manifest that they were not all of us.

20 But ye have an unction from the Holy One, and ye know all things.

21 I have not written unto you because ye know not the truth, but because ye know it, and that no lie is of the truth.

22 Who is a liar but he that denieth that Jesus is the Christ? He is antichrist, that denieth the Father and the Son.

23 Whosoever denieth the Son, the same hath not the Father: .

24 Let that therefore abide in you, which ye have heard from the beginning. If that which ye have heard from

the beginning shall remain in you, ye also shall continue in the Son, and in the Father.

25 And this is the promise that he hath promised us, even eternal life.

26 These things have I written unto you concerning them that seduce you.

27 But the anointing which ye have received of him abideth in you, and ye need not that any man teach you: but as the same anointing teacheth you of all things, and is truth, and is no lie, and even as it hath taught you, ye shall abide in him.

28 And now, little children, abide in him; that, when he shall appear, we may have confidence, and not be ashamed before him at his coming.

29 If ye know that he is righteous, ye know that every one that doeth righteousness is born of him.

Separation unto God

Let's face it, being separated unto the Lord God is an incredibly difficult thing to do. It means death to self, and death to the world. It means picking up the Cross in self-denial daily. It is the death to the Kingdom of self-making no provision for the flesh and giving no place to the devil. It's are rare find when one of God's own is completely sold out to live for the Lord rather than self. That saint has gone into the straight gate, and walks in a narrow way, and few are the children of God who have walked in His way.

Abraham is our example of a man, and his family who separated unto the Lord God.

Hebrews 11:8-10
8 By faith Abraham, when he was called to go out into a place which he should after receive for an inheritance, obeyed; and he went out, not knowing whither he went.
9 By faith he sojourned in the land of promise, as in a strange country, dwelling in tabernacles with Isaac and Jacob, the heirs with him of the same promise:
10 For he looked for a city which hath foundations, whose builder and maker is God.

Notice the cost Abraham had to pay, in order to obey God. Abraham had to leave his father, and nation. Now the cost of leaving your father in Middle Eastern culture was to lose the right of the family inheritance. God had promised Abraham an inheritance but would require Abraham to take his family and go to a land after which Abraham would receive as an inheritance. Basically, God had promised Abraham the right to inherit the earth, and Abraham's Seed also was given the promise. Abraham obeyed God, and went out away from his Father's blessing, and sojourned in the land of promise. Abraham for most of his adult life lived in the wilderness, a strange country dwelling in tents. Abraham had basically a nomadic life even though Abraham was looking the city who builder and maker was God. Abraham was looking for God's inheritance and had to live a separated life in order to qualify for God's blessing.

The cost of separation is built upon absolute trust and dependence upon the Lord God. God had promised Abraham a son, but his wife Sarah was barren. Can you imagine the temptation to believe God Had failed you, when you future heirs cannot even be born because your wife is barren? God waited until Abraham was 100 years old, and physically incapable of having children. Sarah's womb was also dead to having children as she was 90, when the son of promise Isaac was born. God's separation process is to break the nature of depending upon human ability, and to put our trust in God's promise and ability.

You might go an entire lifetime without seeing the fulfillment of God's promise in this age. Abraham never saw the fulfillment of God' s promise in his lifetime.

Hebrews 11:13
13 These all died in faith, not having received the promises, but having seen them afar off, and were persuaded of them, and embraced them, and confessed that they were strangers and pilgrims on the earth.

Abraham and Sarah held on to the promises of God seeing them afar off and were convinced to not give up on God. Living a separated life would cost them their convince as they lived as strangers and pilgrims on a journey towards their inheritance. God would give them the land, they will possess the earth as kings and priests, but first would take the promises of God to their graves. It will not be until the first resurrection when Abraham, Isaac, and Jacob the heirs of God's promised inheritance will raise up from among the dead to possess the land to rule they nations of the earth in their immortal bodies. The Kingdom Age is all about the meek inheriting the earth. Those who were faithful in their obedience to Jesus Christ are then qualified for the next age as a legal heir, joint heirs with Jesus Christ.

The separated life is costly now and appears foolish to the natural man. However, eye has not seen, nor has ear heard, nor has entered into the heart of man, what God has prepared for this who love Him. Only a true sojourner who have set the eyes upon the Lord who seek first the coming Kingdom of Heaven who did not live for the things of this present evil age, really know the true price of a separated life unto God. For straight is the gate and narrow is the way to the Kingdom, and few are they who find it.

Hebrews 11:8-19
8 By faith Abraham, when he was called to go out into a place which he should after receive for an inheritance, obeyed; and he went out, not knowing whither he went. 9 By faith he sojourned in the land of promise, as in a strange country, dwelling in tabernacles with Isaac and Jacob, the heirs with him of the same promise:

10 For he looked for a city which hath foundations, whose builder and maker is God.

11 Through faith also Sara herself received strength to conceive seed, and was delivered of a child when she was past age, because she judged him faithful who had promised.

12 Therefore sprang there even of one, and him as good as dead, so many as the stars of the sky in multitude, and as the sand which is by the sea shore innumerable.

13 These all died in faith, not having received the promises, but having seen them afar off, and were persuaded of them, and embraced them, and confessed that they were strangers and pilgrims on the earth.

14 For they that say such things declare plainly that they seek a country.

15 And truly, if they had been mindful of that country from whence they came out, they might have had opportunity to have returned.

16 But now they desire a better country, that is, an heavenly: wherefore God is not ashamed to be called their God: for he hath prepared for them a city.

17 By faith Abraham, when he was tried, offered up Isaac: and he that had received the promises offered up his only begotten son,

18 Of whom it was said, That in Isaac shall thy seed be called:

19 Accounting that God was able to raise him up, even from the dead; from whence also he received him in a figure.

Warning of End Time Apostasy

The Scriptures point to Christians departing from the faith giving heed to seducing spirits (false teachers) and doctrines of demons. (1 Timothy 4:1) In order for apostasy to happen a person must have first come to a genuine faith, and then walk away or depart from the commitment. Apostasy is when born again Christians who have come to saving faith in Jesus Christ simply walk away, or no longer believe. Now history has proven the Church at large has abandoned the faith, as demonstrated by the dark ages and the false doctrine of the Catholic Church. So, Christians must question can apostasy be happening in our day. Do modern day Christians have the opportunity to walk away from God, or embrace false doctrines and teachers? I want to submit to you; American Christians are deep into spiritual warfare with the antichrist spirit and apostate Christianity.

What happens when Christians follow "another Jesus," or teach another gospel, or are led by another spirit other than the Holy Spirit? What was once the authentic faith, now becomes counterfeit Christianity, "a form of Godliness," but denies the essentials of the faith. The person of Jesus Christ is "no longer God," the gospel is "no longer the Cross," and the Holy Spirit conviction, is eliminated. In its place Christian teachers say Jesus Christ was "just a man": a model to follow, an anointed man in right relationship with God, but not God. The Gospel of the Cross which saves men, is no longer the

Gospel message. Instead a false Gospel which saves the world called the gospel of the Kingdom is now superseding the inferior message of the Cross. Instead of the Holy Spirit being poured out, and bringing conviction of sins, the Church is being taught Jesus Christ did not die for sin to satisfy the wrath of God. In their false Gospel are no more future judgments, no future Hell, all men in the end will be saved.

Now I must ask you, why has the simple Gospel changed so completely within the last 20 years? Is this a picture of the glorious Church advancing the kingdom all over the world, to make Christian cities and nations, as some suggest? Or is this an evidence of a "great end time apostasy from the faith?" Is the Protestant Church now also following in the footsteps of the Catholic Church, by denying the "reformation, with a counter reformation," leading the Church into apostasy? I want to suggest what is called the gospel of the Kingdom, is a denial of the Cross, introduces another Jesus, and is an apostate man glorifying, manmade kingdom building departure from Jesus Christ. At the heart of modern-day apostasy is the glorification of man, which is preparing the way for the coming false Messiah, the Antichrist. When man replaces Jesus Christ as the head of the Church, it is "an abomination which makes desolate;" Jesus Christ left on the outside knocking on the door, being shut out from the Church.

Revelation 3:14-22

14 And unto the angel of the church of the Laodiceans write; These things saith the Amen, the faithful and true witness, the beginning of the creation of God;

15 I know thy works, that thou art neither cold nor hot: I would thou wert cold or hot.

16 So then because thou art lukewarm, and neither cold nor hot, I will spue thee out of my mouth.

17 Because thou sayest, I am rich, and increased with goods, and have need of nothing; and knowest not that thou art wretched, and miserable, and poor, and blind, and naked:

18 I counsel thee to buy of me gold tried in the fire, that thou mayest be rich; and white raiment, that thou mayest be clothed, and that the shame of thy nakedness do not appear; and anoint thine eyes with eyesalve, that thou mayest see.

19 As many as I love, I rebuke and chasten: be zealous therefore, and repent.

20 Behold, I stand at the door, and knock: if any man hear my voice, and open the door, I will come in to him, and will sup with him, and he with me.

21 To him that overcometh will I grant to sit with me in my throne, even as I also overcame, and am set down with my Father in his throne.

22 He that hath an ear, let him hear what the Spirit saith unto the churches.

Chapter 10
Free Gift of Grace and Works of Rewards

Cross and Works of Reward

Every Christian is familiar with the free gift of grace coming from the Cross of Jesus Christ. However few Christians have been taught on works of faith for reward at the Judgment Seat of Christ. The result is when "works" are emphasized in New Testament scripture you get many Christians quoting for by "grace through faith... not by works," as the free gift of salvation. These passages are directly related to the Cross and the judgment Jesus took for all humanity. The mistake comes when Christians try to eliminate "works" after being saved by grace. The Judgment Seat of Christ is a "future judgment" for all saints both Old Testament and New and is based upon works done in our body, both good and bad. The one being judged at Christ's Judgment Seat are "saints only," no one who is "unsaved" will appear at the Judgment Seat.
First Christians are judged by the Cross where Jesus Christ has become our substitute bearing in His body our penalty and punishment for sin. However, our future judgment at the Second Coming of Jesus Christ is "not based" on our salvation as the Cross has "already given" the free gift of grace. Instead our future judgment is what each individual saint has accomplished in "works of faith." The Judgment Seat

instead is for rewards or punishment according to things done after coming to saving faith.

The parable of the 10 talents teaches the truth of future judgment for saints including both rewards and punishment. In this parable the first two servants traded God given talents wisely. Upon the return of Jesus Christ, they were both "rewarded" with entrance into the Kingdom of Heaven and were rewarded many cities to rule with Christ. However, the servant who buried his one talent was reprimanded as a "wicked and unprofitable" servant. This wicked servant was no less a "saint" than the first two, so we must accept the punishment assigned to him as we would accept the rewards of the first two faithful saints. The punishment for the wicked servant was severe as the rewards for the faithful are very great. "Bind that wicked servant hand and foot and cast him in outer darkness where there is weeping and gnashing of teeth."

One might ask how can severe judgment be executed upon a fellow servant and saint of the Lord? At least we could say the wicked saint was not rewarded "entrance into the Kingdom" and was treated like an unbeliever for a period. Did such an unfaithful servant of the Lord lose his salvation? The scriptures teach saints born again of the Holy Spirit at the Judgment Seat are not judged for their salvation, instead are rewarded or punished according to their "works." The fact all Christians will stand to give an account at the end of the age is firmly established throughout the whole of scripture.

Matthew 25: 14-31

14 For the kingdom of heaven is as a man travelling into a far country, who called his own servants, and delivered unto them his goods.

15 And unto one he gave five talents, to another two, and to another one; to every man according to his several ability; and straightway took his journey.

16 Then he that had received the five talents went and traded with the same, and made them other five talents.

17 And likewise he that had received two, he also gained other two.

18 But he that had received one went and digged in the earth, and hid his lord's money.

19 After a long time the lord of those servants cometh, and reckoneth with them.

20 And so he that had received five talents came and brought other five talents, saying, Lord, thou deliveredst unto me five talents: behold, I have gained beside them five talents more.

21 His lord said unto him, Well done, thou good and faithful servant: thou hast been faithful over a few things, I will make thee ruler over many things: enter thou into the joy of thy lord.

22 He also that had received two talents came and said, Lord, thou deliveredst unto me two talents: behold, I have gained two other talents beside them.

23 His lord said unto him, Well done, good and faithful servant; thou hast been faithful over a few things, I will

make thee ruler over many things: enter thou into the joy of thy lord.

24 Then he which had received the one talent came and said, Lord, I knew thee that thou art an hard man, reaping where thou hast not sown, and gathering where thou hast not strawed:

25 And I was afraid, and went and hid thy talent in the earth: lo, there thou hast that is thine.

26 His lord answered and said unto him, Thou wicked and slothful servant, thou knewest that I reap where I sowed not, and gather where I have not strawed:

27 Thou oughtest therefore to have put my money to the exchangers, and then at my coming I should have received mine own with usury.

28 Take therefore the talent from him, and give it unto him which hath ten talents.

29 For unto every one that hath shall be given, and he shall have abundance: but from him that hath not shall be taken away even that which he hath.

30 And cast ye the unprofitable servant into outer darkness: there shall be weeping and gnashing of teeth.

31 When the Son of man shall come in his glory, and all the holy angels with him, then shall he sit upon the throne of his glory:

Why Good Works Are Rejected by Modern Church

The controversy of Christians being excluded from the coming Kingdom age is brought about by Christians not rightly dividing the written Word of God. Usually, the issue of Kingdom exclusion is mixed up with once saved always saved by the Calvinist's, or loss of salvation by Arminianism. However, Kingdom exclusion is neither the loss of salvation or eternal security. Instead the issues being salvation, the doctrine is about rewards at the Second Coming or the loss of rewards. The fact of salvation has already been determined by the Cross as a free gift of grace. So, at the Judgment Seat of Christ "works of faith are measured," and a life of obedient devotion after coming into saving faith. The question of Kingdom of Heaven entrance is one of works for reward independent of the fact the saint has already been saved by grace as a free gift. Scriptures which address disciples of Jesus Christ which speak of good works are not for their salvation, instead are about serving the Lord and being rewarded in the next age. The modern Church has had a difficult time separating passages which speak of the free gift of grace from those which speak of good works for reward. Attempting to downplay passages of Scripture which speak of good works after coming into saving faith will bring about dire consequences for those who are truly saved by grace as Gods free gift of salvation.

Whenever I have brought up conditions required by Scriptures which are "works based, or good works," after coming into saving faith, I usually get rejected for my statements. Why does this happen? The Bible teaches both the free gift of grace, and righteous works for reward. Both are clearly defined by Scriptures, but the modern Church mostly only focuses upon the free gift of grace for salvation. In other words, man cannot in any way add works in order to be saved by grace. No human merit is included in the free gift of grace which has obtained the believers salvation. Here is the Scripture most often quoted which goes in line with grace without works to be saved.

Ephesians 2:8-9
8 For by grace are ye saved through faith; and that not of yourselves: it is the gift of God:
9 Not of works, lest any man should boast.

Now being saved by grace without any human merit is the foundation of the Christian faith. This is all accomplished by Jesus Christ on the Cross and in His resurrection as the work of redemption. Nothing can be added or subtracted from what Christ has already done in saving grace. When the Scriptures then speak of living holy righteous lives the ability has come from the free gift of grace making new creations out of sinful man. Kingdom exclusion does not invalidate the Cross or add or subtract from salvation in Christ alone. Instead acknowledges the Cross has judged our sin and given the man who received Jesus Christ forgiveness of sin, and eternal life. A Christian who has lost the Kingdom has lost their reward of inheritance but maintains eternal life.

This position in Scriptures is difficult for many Christians to believe as they have been wrongly taught the Kingdom of Heaven is already qualified for their entrance simply as a free gift of grace by the work of the Cross. As I have endeavored to demonstrate the great volume of Scriptures which warn Christians of Kingdom exclusion, the Cross clearly has not given the Kingdom as a free gift of grace. Instead the great volume of Scriptures which point to righteous works for reward are about the kingdom age, and the inheritance of the kingdom by qualification. Of course, this brings about anxiety among many professors of the faith as they simply cannot separate the two and mix Scriptures of free grace with works of reward making all say works are not necessary for salvation. At this point the clear separation is dragged into a quagmire mire of debate which has to do with salvation, and not rewards or their loss. Simply put a man can be saved by grace, and still lose the Kingdom but retain eternal life. The loss is one of the Kingdom through a life of unrighteous, a deficiency of not living right with God after coming into saving faith. A fear of Christians being exposed and disinherited at the Judgment Seat causes the debate to flow into eternal security or loss of salvation. Instead of seeing a clear division of loss of Kingdom and eternal rewards.

So with the high anxiety produced by Kingdom Exclusion Scriptures I desire to present a great volume of passages which do demonstrate good works are necessary.

Here are the facts of Scriptures which demonstrates Christians in fact will judged according to their works after coming into saving faith. At this point little regard is given to the responsibility of maintaining good works and being zealous for good works for fear of introducing man made elements into salvation. However, Jesus Christ said of all 7 Churches in the Book of Revelation "I know your works." At the Judgement Seat of Christ every Christian must stand to give account for the things done in their body after coming into saving faith. Things done both good and bad.

God is not a respecter of persons, who will judge everyman according to their works. For those who are luke warm, Jesus Christ will spew them out. For those who defile the Church, Christ will reject them for rewards condemning their actions as "workers of iniquity." The Parables of Talents, Pound, and 10 Virgins are all works based. Each man is rewarded according to what they did or did not do. For some Christians the loss of reward will result in being shut out of the Kingdom and cast into Outer Darkness.

Now notice all these Scriptures which emphasize works of faith after being saved by grace:

Romans 2:9-11
9 Tribulation and anguish, upon every soul of man that doeth evil, of the Jew first, and also of the Gentile; 10 But glory, honour, and peace, to every man that

worketh good, to the Jew first, and also to the Gentile:
11 For there is no respect of persons with God.

The apostle Paul in his letter to the Romans writes
about how God is an impartial judge giving to every man
according to their works. For God is not a respecter of
persons. As stated before a man who seeks glory,
honor, and peace with God will demonstrate a life of
the love of Jesus Christ by keeping His commandments.
A life of Faith has corresponding actions which
demonstrate a devotion to Jesus Christ.

1 Corinthians 3:13-14
13 Every man's work shall be made manifest: for the
day shall declare it, because it shall be revealed by fire;
and the fire shall try every man's work of what sort it is.
14 If any man's work abide which he hath built
thereupon, he shall receive a reward.

As mentioned earlier the Judgment Seat of Christ
written by Paul in his letter to the Church. The day
which declare every man's works is the Day of Judgment
for the saints at the Second Coming of the Lord. Works
are tried in the Judicial Fires of Christ, the Bema, the
Judgment Seat. Works which are burned up have no
reward, their material is manmade and refused by
Christ.

Philippians 2:12
12 Wherefore, my beloved, as ye have always obeyed, not as in my presence only, but now much more in my absence, work out your own salvation with fear and trembling.

The salvation Paul is asking Christian to work out is works of faith and obedience, after coming into saving faith in Christ. Once again works are required by Christians after receiving the free gift of grace, but not to add or subtract from the Cross. The works speak of our agreement to Gods will and way, and our conformity to Christ in acts of practical righteousness.

Colossians 1:10
10 That ye might walk worthy of the Lord unto all pleasing, being fruitful in every good work, and increasing in the knowledge of God;

Fruitful works which please the Lord is a walk of faith and obedience in this present evil age. As noted before Christians can walk after the flesh and are in danger; "will not inherit the Kingdom of Heaven." For without faith is impossible to please God, for whatever is not of faith is sin.

1 Thessalonians 1:3
3 Remembering without ceasing your work of faith, and labour of love, and patience of hope in our Lord Jesus Christ, in the sight of God and our Father;

Paul's letter to the saints of Thessalonians is an encouragement in the face of persecution. Paul must remind them of the Second Coming of Jesus Christ and the Coming Kingdom Age. Some may have feared the "catching up of the saints," so Paul encourages them the time of the Tribulation is still future. Even though they were suffering great persecution, Paul exhorts them about their works of faith, and labor of love. Paul commends their service in the Lord which includes works after coming into saving faith.

2 Thessalonians 2:17
17 Comfort your hearts, and stablish you in every good word and work.

Paul in his second letter to Thessalonians gives a detailed account of the events which preceded the Second Coming of Jesus Christ. Paul warns of great apostasy from the faith at that time and exhorts the saints how the Lord was establishing them in good works.

1 Timothy 2:9-10
9 In like manner also, that women adorn themselves in modest apparel, with shamefacedness and sobriety; not with braided hair, or gold, or pearls, or costly array;
10 But (which becometh women professing godliness) with good works.

In this letter to Timothy Paul demonstrates how works of the Lord include holiness, and practical righteous living. Once again works are not to save or to add to the Cross instead our works of righteousness which is required of the Bride of Christ.

1 Timothy 5:24-25
24 Some men's sins are open beforehand, going before to judgment; and some men they follow after.
25 Likewise also the good works of some are manifest beforehand; and they that are otherwise cannot be hid.

Paul teaches about the qualifications of elders who lead the local Church. Paul speaks of Gods judgment with Church elders, some sins going before in judgement while others will have their sins uncovered at the Judgment Seat of Christ. Also says the same about their good works which are seen now, and others good works will be clearly seen when revealed by the Lord.

1 Timothy 6:17-19
17 Charge them that are rich in this world, that they be not high minded, nor trust in uncertain riches, but in the living God, who giveth us richly all things to enjoy;
18 That they do good, that they be rich in good works, ready to distribute, willing to communicate;
19 Laying up in store for themselves a good foundation against the time to come, that they may lay hold on eternal life.

Paul tells Timothy to warn Christians who are rich in the worlds goods to lay up a good foundation against the time to come. Meaning their righteous acts, their good works is about their willingness to distribute their wealth to help those saints in need. Giving by those who are rich is considered good works by the Lord when accompanied by pure motives. At the Judgement Seat, the giving of the wealthy can be judged by the Lord as works of righteousness. Laying up treasure in heaven by being willing to communicate their wealth in service to the Lord.

2 Timothy 3:16-17
16 All scripture is given by inspiration of God, and is profitable for doctrine, for reproof, for correction, for instruction in righteousness:
17 That the man of God may be perfect, throughly furnished unto all good works.

Paul instructs Timothy those who study to show themselves approved of the Lord can instruct the Church in the doctrines of Christ. All Scripture has been given by God and ministering the Word of God brings profit in doctrine, reproof, and correction in righteousness. Leaders who teach the Word of God will be tried at the Judgment Seat, those who are proficient will be judged for their good works in teaching the true doctrines of the Lord.

Titus 2:7
7 In all things shewing thyself a pattern of good works:
in doctrine shewing incorruptness, gravity, sincerity,

In the body of Christ, young men are exhorted to show a
pattern of good works. In doctrine showing purity,
honesty, and genuineness. Shows how much the
preaching of the Gospel is considered a good work of
the Lord.

Titus 2:13-15
13 Looking for that blessed hope, and the glorious
appearing of the great God and our Saviour Jesus Christ;
14 Who gave himself for us, that he might redeem us
from all iniquity, and purify unto himself a peculiar
people, zealous of good works.
 15 These things speak, and exhort, and rebuke with all
authority. Let no man despise thee.

Looking for the Blessed Hope means Christ's blessing of
the Second Coming. In the meantime a work of
sanctification among Gods people is ongoing. A peculiar
people separated unto the Lord seeking first the coming
Kingdom of Heaven age. The Lord will have separated
from Himself out from the whole Church a Bride which
has been zealous for good works.

Titus 3:14
14 And let ours also learn to maintain good works for
necessary uses, that they be not unfruitful.

Good works must be maintained by the saints after coming into saving faith. Without good works the saints will be barren and unfruitful having nothing to be rewarded at the Judgment Seat of Christ.

Hebrews 6:10-12
   10 For God is not unrighteous to forget your work and labour of love, which ye have shewed toward his name, in that ye have ministered to the saints, and do minister.
   11 And we desire that every one of you do shew the same diligence to the full assurance of hope unto the end:
   12 That ye be not slothful, but followers of them who through faith and patience inherit the promises.

The book of Hebrews teaches a lot about the future inheritance of rewards or their loss. Every saint is exhorted to show diligence in severing the Lord by good works of faith. Not to be slothful but follow the example of the Old Testament saints who through faith and patience have inherited Gods promises of Kingdom age rewards.

Hebrews 10:24-25
24 And let us consider one another to provoke unto love and to good works:

25 Not forsaking the assembling of ourselves together, as the manner of some is; but exhorting one another: and so much the more, as ye see the day approaching.

Christians are to provoke one another to good works knowing the coming Judgement Seat of Christ, and qualification the Kingdom by works. Especially as the saints see the day of the Lords return where the Church will be tried with apostasy.

Hebrews 1:21
21 Make you perfect in every good work to do his will, working in you that which is well pleasing in his sight, through Jesus Christ; to whom be glory for ever and ever. Amen.

Works of faith after being saved by grace makes for the maturing or perfection of the saints. God works with the saints are to make perfect in every good work the saint who is willing to surrender to His will. For without faith it is impossible to please Him, as the Lord is a rewarder of those who diligently seek Him.

James 2:14-26
14 What doth it profit, my brethren, though a man say he hath faith, and have not works? can faith save him?
15 If a brother or sister be naked, and destitute of daily food,
16 And one of you say unto them, Depart in peace, be ye warmed and filled; notwithstanding ye give them not

those things which are needful to the body; what doth it profit?

17 Even so faith, if it hath not works, is dead, being alone.

18 Yea, a man may say, Thou hast faith, and I have works: shew me thy faith without thy works, and I will shew thee my faith by my works.

19 Thou believest that there is one God; thou doest well: the devils also believe, and tremble.

20 But wilt thou know, O vain man, that faith without works is dead?

21 Was not Abraham our father justified by works, when he had offered Isaac his son upon the altar?

22 Seest thou how faith wrought with his works, and by works was faith made perfect?

23 And the scripture was fulfilled which saith, Abraham believed God, and it was imputed unto him for righteousness: and he was called the Friend of God.

24 Ye see then how that by works a man is justified, and not by faith only.

25 Likewise also was not Rahab the harlot justified by works, when she had received the messengers, and had sent them out another way?

26 For as the body without the spirit is dead, so faith without works is dead also.

The book of James is one of the overwhelming Scriptural proofs good works must follow the free gift of grace. What is interesting with this passage is the word justification which normally appears with the work of the Cross of Jesus Christ. In legal terms our debut to sin has been paid in full by the substitutionary sacrifice of Jesus Christ who was made sin for us. Upon the resurrection of Jesus Christ all who have faith in Christ are declared justified by faith without works of any kind, or any human merit. Now James introduces another aspect for those who are of the faith; "you see then how that by works a man is justified, and not by faith only." (James 2:24)

The Scriptures point out how Abraham had received the Son of Promise Isaac, offered Isaac back to the Lord as a blood sacrifice at the Lords direction to obey the giving of Isaac as a sacrifice on an alter at Mount Moriah. Abraham believed God taking Isaac to Mount Moriah and placing upon Isaac upon the alter raising his knife to slay the Son of Promise Isaac. God at that point intervened stopping Abraham from slaying Isaac and provided a lamb as the blood sacrifice. A foreshadowing the sacrifice of Jesus Christ as the Lamb of God who takes away the sin of the world. In this case Abraham must act in obedience to the Lords command as a work of faith.

When Abraham acted in faith it was considered a work of righteousness, and God imputed unto Abraham for righteousness, and Abraham at that point was declared the friend of God. This action taken by Abraham in obedience to Christ's command was what justified Abraham before God. This kind of justification is not what is given as a free gift where God does all the work and men are the recipients of free grace. This justification does not determine our standing before the Lord, as only the Blood of the Cross can give us justification from our sin. Instead this justification is all about our obedience after coming into saving faith and is relegated to eternal rewards and blessing. As demonstrated before you can be saved and still be lacking in works of faith or live after the flesh and be disinherited for Kingdom entrance and rewards. As the body without the spirit is dead, so is faith without works dead also. (James 2:26)

In the Scriptures two types of justification and two types of righteousness are written. If Christians don't properly divide the Scriptures, they will miss the mark of the true meaning of works of faith after being saved by grace. Not works to justify our salvation, instead works of faith which is measured as obedience to Christ's commands. A righteousness from the Cross given as a free gift making the saints holy, blameless, and irretrievable in Gods sight. Also, a righteousness which comes from obedience to Christ's commands after being saved by grace. Which are works of faith our righteous acts to be measured at the Judgment Seat of Christ.

1 Peter 1:15-17
15 But as he which hath called you is holy, so be ye holy in all manner of conversation;
16 Because it is written, Be ye holy; for I am holy.

17 And if ye call on the Father, who without respect of persons judgeth according to every man's work, pass the time of your sojourning here in fear:

Once again, another original apostle confirms the necessity of righteous holy living to be judged at the Second Coming of Jesus Christ. Every man's work will be judged by God without respect of persons. Works will merit rewards in the Kingdom age if they pass through the judicial fires of the Christ's measurement. Knowing holiness is required to enter the coming Kingdom of Heaven age, we need to pass out time of sojourning hear in fear.

Revelation 2:23
23 And I will kill her children with death; and all the churches shall know that I am he which searcheth the reins and hearts: and I will give unto every one of you according to your works.

Judgment of God is pronounced upon corruption in the Church, as God searches out the thoughts and intents of our hearts and actions. Once again God promises to judge everyman without respect of persons according to their works.

Revelation 3:16-17
15 I know thy works, that thou art neither cold nor hot: I would thou wert cold or hot.

16 So then because thou art lukewarm, and neither cold nor hot, I will spew thee out of my mouth.

The Seven Churches of Asia are a good representation of warning. Here the Church of Laodicea is deceived to think the worlds riches are a sign of God's blessing. Instead the worlds good had drawn them away from the Lord into being luke warm in their commitment to Jesus Christ. The Church has been judged by Christ according to their works and would be spewed out by the Lord as their actions left a bad taste in judgment.

Revelation 20:13-15
13 And the sea gave up the dead which were in it; and death and hell delivered up the dead which were in them: and they were judged every man according to their works.
14 And death and hell were cast into the lake of fire. This is the second death.
15 And whosoever was not found written in the book of life was cast into the lake of fire.

In the Book of Revelation two resurrections are recorded separated by one thousand years. The first resurrection is of the righteous dead in Christ who qualified for the Kingdom age. The Second Resurrection is after the Kingdom age, and all other men are judged according to their works at the Great White Throne of God. Every man is rewarded or punished according to what they have done. Whosoever was not found written in the Book of Life was cast into the Lake of Fire which is the Second Death as it occurs after man is raised from the dead.

Revelation 22:12
12 And, behold, I come quickly; and my reward is with me, to give every man according as his work shall be.

God promises to come quickly, and His reward is with Him at His coming. To give to everyman according to what he has done in his lifetime.

Scriptures on Reward

Matthew 5:12
12 Rejoice, and be exceeding glad: for great is your reward in heaven: for so persecuted they the prophets which were before you.

The Sermon on the Mount as spoken by Jesus Christ has much to say about righteous living and rewards. Concerning Christians being persecuted for righteous holy living as a witness for Jesus Christ. Jesus proclaims to the suffers their reward will be great. For so had the prophets of the Lord suffered for the faith when they withstood ungodliness' in their days.

Matthew 5:46
46 For if ye love them which love you, what reward
have ye? do not even the publicans the same?

In the Sermon on the Mount Jesus Christ spoke of loving
your enemies, and blessing those who curse you, and
praying for those who despitefully use you. For what
reward is there in the Coming Kingdom Age of only
loving those who love you.

Matthew 6:1-5
1 Take heed that ye do not your alms before men, to be
seen of them: otherwise ye have no reward of your
Father which is in heaven.
2 Therefore when thou doest thine alms, do not sound a
trumpet before thee, as the hypocrites do in the
synagogues and in the streets, that they may have glory
of men. Verily I say unto you, They have their reward.
3 But when thou doest alms, let not thy left hand know
what thy right hand doeth:
4 That thine alms may be in secret: and thy Father
which seeth in secret himself shall reward thee openly.
5 And when thou prayest, thou shalt not be as the
hypocrites are: for they love to pray standing in the
synagogues and in the corners of the streets, that they
may be seen of men. Verily I say unto you, They have
their reward.
6 But thou, when thou prayest, enter into thy closet,
and when thou hast shut thy door, pray to thy Father

which is in secret; and thy Father which seeth in secret shall reward thee openly.

The Sermon on the Mount also address works which are done to receive glory from men.
Praying on street corners like a Pharisee to gain the approval of man will not be rewarded by God. Instead Christ spoke of a hidden life of devotion, hidden from the view and praise of man. Praying in Secret will in the future lead to Kingdom age rewards. Many will exchange the praise of God for the praise of man. The worlds accolades and riches will be that man's rewards in exchange for the praise and glory of God. For those who compromise with manmade glory they have their "rewards now."

Matthew 6:16-18
16 Moreover when ye fast, be not, as the hypocrites, of a sad countenance: for they disfigure their faces, that they may appear unto men to fast. Verily I say unto you, They have their reward.
17 But thou, when thou fastest, anoint thine head, and wash thy face;
18 That thou appear not unto men to fast, but unto thy Father which is in secret: and thy Father, which seeth in secret, shall reward thee openly.

For those who seek man's glory they fast to be seen of men. For those who fast for God in secret the Lord will openly reward them in the future Kingdom of Heaven Age.

Matthew 10:40-41
40 He that receiveth you receiveth me, and he that receiveth me receiveth him that sent me.
41 He that receiveth a prophet in the name of a prophet shall receive a prophet's reward; and he that receiveth a righteous man in the name of a righteous man shall receive a righteous man's reward.

The Lord Jesus Christ commissioned his apostles to go forth and announce the Kingdom of Heaven was at hand. For those who received those who were sent by the Lord would receive a reward from accepting Christ's messengers. Jesus Christ went on to say receiving the Lords prophet would come with the blessing of receiving a prophet's reward. A reward would be obtained by receiving a righteous man, instead of rejecting or persecuting the Lords servants.

Matthew 16:27
27 For the Son of man shall come in the glory of his Father with his angels; and then he shall reward every man according to his works.

The time of the Lords rewards is clearly stated in this passage. At the time of Jesus Christ return with His heavenly angels, then shall Jesus Christ reward everyman according to their works.

1 Corinthians 3:8-15
8 Now he that planteth and he that watereth are one:
and every man shall receive his own reward according
to his own labour.
9 For we are labourers together with God: ye are God's
husbandry, ye are God's building.
10 According to the grace of God which is given unto
me, as a wise master builder, I have laid the foundation,
and another buildeth thereon. But let every man take
heed how he buildeth thereupon.
11 For other foundation can no man lay than that is laid,
which is Jesus Christ.
12 Now if any man build upon this foundation gold,
silver, precious stones, wood, hay, stubble;
13 Every man's work shall be made manifest: for the
day shall declare it, because it shall be revealed by fire;
and the fire shall try every man's work of what sort it is.
14 If any man's work abide which he hath built
thereupon, he shall receive a reward.
15 If any man's work shall be burned, he shall suffer
loss: but he himself shall be saved; yet so as by fire.

The process by which Christians will give an account as
to how they lived their lives after coming into saving
faith is clearly written by apostle Paul in his first letter to
the Church of Corinth. The judicial fire of Christ's
judgment Seat will test the quality of every Christian
work. For those who have the judicial fires approve of
their works they shall receive Kingdom age rewards. For

those who have their works burned up, they have no reward, and no Kingdom Heaven entrance.

1 Corinthians 9:17-18
17 For if I do this thing willingly, I have a reward: but if against my will, a dispensation of the gospel is committed unto me.
18 What is my reward then? Verily that, when I preach the gospel, I may make the gospel of Christ without charge, that I abuse not my power in the gospel.

Apostle Paul's reward was based upon Paul fulfilling his commission from God.

Colossians 2:18
18 Let no man beguile you of your reward in a voluntary humility and worshipping of angels, intruding into those things which he hath not seen, vainly puffed up by his fleshly mind,

Notice the danger which the Apostle Paul warns the Church, another man can rob you from your reward by deceiving the saints to act outside authentic works of faith. It is sad to think how many Christians are following the seducing spirits of false teachers, and their doctrines of demons. How sad will be the day of a deceived saint who followed a man into deception and cost him his Kingdom age inheritance.

Colossians 3:24
24 Knowing that of the Lord ye shall receive the reward of the inheritance: for ye serve the Lord Christ.

Don't serve men who can only reward you with the world's riches. Instead seek first the Kingdom of Heaven, for from the Lord shall the faithful saints receive the reward of the inheritance.

2 Timothy 4:14
14 Alexander the coppersmith did me much evil: the Lord reward him according to his works:

Apostle Paul suffered greatly at the hands of Alexander the coppersmith. Paul has entrusted his life in the face of martyrdom. Paul knew the Lord would reward Alexander his persecution of Paul and the Lords Church.

Hebrews 2:2
2 For if the word spoken by angels was stedfast, and every transgression and disobedience received a just recompence of reward;

The Hebrews writer is warning Christians God will not overlook any man's acts of sin or disobedience. For every transgressions and act against God in disobedience in Israel's wilderness journey was judged by God and received a just recompense of reward. In many cases their action lead to Gods anger, and even death.

Hebrews 10:35
35 Cast not away therefore your confidence, which hath great recompense of reward.

The Hebrews writer was warning Christians against the sin of apostasy. For in falling away from the faith is to cast away your future inheritance into the Kingdom Age.

Hebrews 11:6
6 But without faith it is impossible to please him: for he that cometh to God must believe that he is, and that he is a rewarder of them that diligently seek him.

In the Book of Hebrews Old Testament saints who acquired Kingdom Age rewards is listed. By no means is list exhaustive, rather an example of a few who were more notable in Israel's development and history. Acts of authentic faith in obedience to God are recorded as our example upon whom the end of the age has come.

Hebrews 11:26
26 Esteeming the reproach of Christ greater riches than the treasures in Egypt: for he had respect unto the recompense of the reward.

Moses was able to refuse being the next King of the world, and to choose to suffer reproach with the people of God. Moses was able to let go of the world's riches, glory, and fame, for Moses had respect unto Gods future rewards.

2 Peter 2:13
13 And shall receive the reward of unrighteousness, as they that count it pleasure to riot in the day time. Spots they are and blemishes, sporting themselves with their own deceivings while they feast with you;

Apostle Peter warns the false prophets who are deceiving the Church will receive the reward of the unrighteous. For sure will be shut out of the Kingdom Age entrance and are likely to be pronounced wicked and profitable servants. To be cast into outer darkness where there will be weeping and gnashing of the teeth.

2 John 1:8
8 Look to yourselves, that we lose not those things which we have wrought, but that we receive a full reward.

The Apostle John demonstrates they are different levels of Kingdom Age rewards. John exhorts the saints to watch over their lives so as not to lose the rewards they have already worked so hard for. Instead must continue unto the end to receive "a full reward."

Jude1:11
11 Woe unto them! for they have gone in the way of Cain, and ran greedily after the error of Balaam for reward, and perished in the gainsaying of Core.

False prophets have crept into the Church. Jude warns these men are likened unto the false prophet Balaam from the Old Testament. These false prophets are greedy and want to exploit the Church for personal profit and riches. We must remember the Lord uses a donkey to rebuke the madness of Balaam the false prophet.

Revelation 11:18
18 And the nations were angry, and thy wrath is come, and the time of the dead, that they should be judged, and that thou shouldest give reward unto thy servants the prophets, and to the saints, and them that fear thy name, small and great; and shouldest destroy them which destroy the earth.

The time of rewarding the prophets of the Lord is given in this passage in the Book of Revelation. John also writes of rewards being given to all saints who qualify both small and great.

Revelation 22:12
12 And, behold, I come quickly; and my reward is with me, to give every man according as his work shall be.

One of the final passage of Scriptures is the promise of the soon return of Jesus Christ. The rewards of the Lord come with the Lord as they are for the faithful saints throughout all human time in this present evil age. Who qualified by their faithful obedience to God during their lifetimes?

Conclusion

I have provided the writings of many historic teachers who held the position of Kingdom of Heaven exclusion. My hope is those who have read this book and are struggling with its conclusions will continue further in the study of Kingdom of Heaven teachings from others who have written in the past.

GH Lang

The connection between sharing the sufferings of our Lord and sharing His glory was never more distinctly stated than by Himself when answering the two disciples who requested to be assured that they should sit on His right hand and left hand in His glory. To these aspirants for chief honors Christ most significantly replied, "Ye know not what ye ask"; and the context shows that their ignorance lay, not in their not having some sense of the greatness of the desired honour, but in their not appreciating the price to be paid in suffering with Him if such dignity was to be attained; for, He added, "Are ye able to drink the cup that I drink? or to be baptized with the baptism with which I am baptized?" And our Lord strikingly showed that in such matters there is to be no favoritism by adding that "to sit on My right hand or on My left hand is not Mine to give, but to them for whom it hath been prepared" (Mark 10: 37-40).

It is in line with this that authority over the nations, and sharing the regal glories of the Lord, are promised to "conquerers," as in Rev. 2: 26, 27, and 3: 21. This latter verse reads: "He that overcometh, I will give to him to sit down with me in my throne, as I also overcame, and sat down with my Father in his throne"; and the words "even as I also conquered" firmly establish the parallel between Christ and His people in the matter of the condition upon which they, as He, must attain to the throne. Alas, that these words of an old writer should still be true of so many: "Jesus has now many lovers of His heavenly kingdom, but few bearers of His cross. He finds many companions of His table, but few of His fasting. Many follow Jesus as far as the breaking of bread, but few to the drinking of the chalice of His passion."

It was Paul's yearning to follow the Lamb whithersoever He went. Writing to the Philippians he states very powerfully the distinction between the righteousness which justifies [by faith] before God, in which no works of ours have the slightest part, and that full knowledge of the Lord by the justified one which will ensure a full reward. He says:-

"Howbeit what things were gain to me, these have I counted loss for Christ. Yea verily, and I count all things to be loss for the excellency of the knowledge of Christ Jesus my Lord: for whom I suffered the loss of all things, and do count them but dung, that I may gain Christ and be found in him, not having a righteousness of mine own, even that which is of the law, but that which is through faith in Christ, the righteousness which is of God by faith: that I may know him, and the power of his resurrection, and the fellowship of his sufferings, becoming conformed unto his death; if by any means I may attain unto the resurrection from the dead. Not that I have already obtained, or am already made perfect: but I press on, if so he that I may lay hold of that for which also I was laid hold of by Christ Jesus. Brethren, I count not myself yet to have laid hold: but one thing I do, forgetting the things which are behind, and stretching forward to the things which are before, I press on toward the goal unto the prize of the high calling of God in Christ Jesus. Let us therefore, as many as be perfect [full-grown] be thus minded: and if in anything ye are otherwise minded, even this shall God reveal unto you: only, whereunto we have already attained, by that same rule let us walk" (Phil. 3: 7-16).

The being raised in the first resurrection assures a place in the [millennial] kingdom, and honour therein; and such as are not then raised will miss that kingly glory, since the second and las resurrection is not to take place till after the millennial period (Rev. 20: 4-6). On the other hand, those who attain to that kingship will retain it for ever, and not cease to reign at the end of the thousand years, for it is written concerning such that "they shall reign for ever and ever" (Rev. 22: 5). From which it would appear that those who enter the [eternal] kingdom [in 'a new heaven and a new earth' (Rev. 21: 1)] at the close of the millennial period will not attain to kingly dignity therein, since that is stated only of those who had reached the bridal glory, the members of the Jerusalem which is above. It thus becomes a matter of everlasting consequence to be of those who participate in the first resurrection. (First Born Sons Their Rights and Risks Chapter 8: The First Resurrection A Prize)

Pastor B Herrell
"One of the major themes throughout The Scriptures is the coming of our Lord and His Messianic Kingdom (Isaiah 9: 6, 7, 11; Jeremiah 23: 5, 6; Ezekiel 37: 15-28; Daniel 2: 44; 7: 9-27; Zechariah 14: 9).

In view of the coming kingdom, the author of Hebrews exhorts his readers to remain faithful to their Lord so that they do not forfeit their inheritance. This inheritance includes sharing in the first resurrection, being joint-heirs with Christ, serving as priests to God and being citizens of the new Jerusalem.

Because of the potential for his readers to miss out in their inheritance in the coming kingdom, the author includes five warning passages in his letter. These passages are written to remind the believers of the rewards for faithfulness and the severe consequences for turning away from Christ. ...

The fact that Jesus the Messiah is the Davidic King and Heir is stated throughout Chapter one by the author as he quotes from six Messianic Psalms (2: 7; 104: 4; 45: 6, 7; 102: 25-27; 110: 1; 8: 4, 6) and the Davidic Covenant (2 Samuel 7: 14; 1Chronicles 17: 13). These quotations from the Psalms state that Jesus is the Son of David and God's chosen Heir. He is going to defeat His enemies when He returns to set up His Kingdom and rule over the earth. ...

These Messianic Psalms guarantee final fulfilment when our Lord returns and sets up His Kingdom on the earth. Everyone who remains faithful to the Lord will be joint-heirs with Christ in the Kingdom of God. The author of Hebrews does not want his readers to be excluded from the Messianic Kingdom. Becoming companions with Christ and ruling with Him in the Kingdom of God is the 'great salvation' in verse three, which they cannot afford to ignore. ...

"Further conformation of the coming Kingdom is the outpouring of God the Holy Spirit after our Lord's enthronement by God the Father. The outpouring of

the Holy Spirit included 'signs, wonders and various miracles' by the apostles (Acts 2: 43), 'and gifts of the Holy Spirit' (1 Corinthians 12: 4-7, 11; 1 Peter 4: 10, 11). The giving of the Holy Spirit is a spiritual blessing of the Kingdom of God under the New Covenant (Romans 14: 17; 2 Corinthians 3: 1-6) and is the down payment guaranteeing that the rest of the kingdom blessings will come when the Lord returns (2 Corinthians 1: 22; Ephesians 1: 11-14; Thessalonians 1: 3-7). Today we live during the mystery or inaugural phase of the Kingdom. This began with our Lord's First Advent and will reach its completion at the end of this age with the harvest of the righteous and the wicked (Matthew 13: 24-30, 36-43). In this inaugural phase of the Kingdom, our King is seated in heaven and the righteous serve Him on earth as His ambassadors (2 Corinthians 5: 20; Colossians 1: 12-14). When our Lord returns at the end of this age, He will set up the Kingdom of Heaven on the earth. He will then rule on the earth with the righteous for one thousand years (Revelation 20: 4-6)."
(PASTOR B. HERRELL Pressing On Towards the Prize; themillennialkingdom.org.uk)

Dr. AB Simpson
"The Holy Spirit prepares us for the coming of the Lord, and to be among 'the first fruits' at His appearing. There is a remarkable expression in Romans 8: 23, which has a deeper meaning than the first fruits of the Spirit. It means that the Holy Spirit is preparing a first company of holy and consecrated hearts for the coming

of the Lord and the gathering of His saints, and that these will be followed later by the larger company of all the saved. There is a first resurrection, in which the blessed and holy shall have part, and of this He is preparing all who are willing to receive Him in His fulness. Transcendent honour! Unspeakable privilege! May God enable us to have a part in that blessed hope!" (AB Simpson: Pressing On Towards the Prize; themillennialkingdom.org.uk)

Jesse Penn Lewis
"The millennial throne of Christ is to be shared with others on certain conditions, by the gift of Christ Himself. 'I will give to him to sit with Me.' Paul refers to this heirship in his unfolding of the work of the Holy Spirit in Rom. 8. 'Joint-heirs with Christ ... if so be that we suffer with Him' (Rom. 8: 17). This is foreshadowed in Daniel 7: 22-27, where it says, 'the time came that the saints possessed the kingdom.' The fact that Christ's coming throne is to be shared by overcomers, who are appointed by the Father to be 'joint-heirs' with Him, who was 'appointed heir of all things,' is therefore quite clear.

Glimpses are to be found, too, into the future time when the Christ, and those who are to share the throne with Him, will reign. Paul said: 'Know ye not that the saints shall judge the world?' 'Know ye not that we shall judge angels?' (1Cor. 6: 2,3). What angels? Certainly not the unfallen ones. The explanation will be found in 2 Peter 2: 4. "The angels which kept not their first estate ... judged." These fallen angels - Satan and his hierarchy of evil powers - are to be judged by those who reign with Christ on His throne. In brief, they who are 'overcomers' - those who overcome the world and Satan now will be the 'judges' of the fallen hosts of evil, when these overcoming ones are 'glorified together' with Christ upon His throne.

The obtaining of the prize of this 'high calling' of sharing the Throne with Christ was the incentive which urged Paul on to count all things loss to obtain it, and to be willing to be made conformable to the death of Christ as the primary means for reaching such an end (see Phil. 3: 10-14); for each believer who reaches the prize of the throne, goes by way of the Cross in the path of the Ascended Lord.
(Jesse Penn Lewis: Pressing On Towards the Prize; themillennialkingdom.org.uk)

Robert Govett

Excerpt from 2nd Letter To Molesworth answering objections to Christians being excluded from coming Kingdom of Heaven.

2. You strangely cite 1Cor. 6: 9-11. This is the stronghold of our doctrine: force this, and I suppose, no other text will stand the shock! First, Paul is addressing in this epistle all believers everywhere: 1 Cor. 1: Next, in

the sixth chapter, he is rebuking those in communion for not settling their disputes among themselves: ver. 1-7. Were not the saints, by God's decree, hereafter to be judges of the world and of angels? Why, then, should they not be able to decide now questions about pounds, shillings, and pence? "But brother goeth to law with brother, and that before the unbelievers." Here the brethren of Corinth are distinguished as believers: those of the world being unbelievers. They ought rather to suffer injustice than bring actions before the world. But some of them, instead of suffering wrong, were inflicting it, and defrauding even their brethren! Then comes the Spirit's rebuke: "Know ye not that unrighteous* [*No article] (ones) shall not inherit (obtain) the kingdom of God? Be not deceived: neither fornicators, nor idolaters, nor adulterers, nor effeminate, nor abusers of themselves with mankind, nor thieves, nor covetous, nor drunkards, nor revilers, nor extortioners, shall inherit the kingdom of God. And such were some of you: but ye were washed, but ye were sanctified, but ye were justified† in the name of the Lord Jesus, and by the Spirit of our God."

[†In the Greek these are Aorists. See also Alford.]

That these threatenings refer to believers seems to me to be certain.
(1) It cannot be said, 'Paul intends certain hypocrites who had crept in among them.' For he says of them all, that they had been justified, sanctified, and baptized.

Can that be true of hypocrites? Some, indeed insist on the words – "Such were some of you." But they are not meant to contradict what Paul had expressly asserted in ver. 8, that some were defrauding and inflicting wrong upon their brethren. It is on the ground of this charge, that he utters the solemn threat which follows.

(2) How stands the apostle's rebuke, if we read it on the usual theory? 'O Christian believers, some of you are defrauding your brethren. What! Do you not know that unconverted men, if unrighteous, shall not enter the kingdom! Do not mistake! No unconverted men, if fornicators or adulterers, will enter that kingdom.' Was that the apostle's meaning? Does he teach that unconverted men, if they are morally decent, will enter the kingdom? I suppose none will say so. Will not unconverted men, simply as unconverted, be refused any portion there? Is not that what Jesus says to Nicodemus? John 3: 3.

But there was, there is great danger, lest those who believe should rest upon their privileges given of God, and suppose that, because admitted to the Church of Christ - because elect, and made the children of God, the Most High would overlook in them what, if done by the ungodly, he would severely punish. From false ideas of Christian liberty, Corinthian Christians were acting quite contrary to the word of Jesus. Is there no danger in this direction in our day? To whom are Paul's "Know ye not?"s addressed, but to believers? Rom. 6: 16; 11: 2; 1 Cor. 3: 16; 5: 6; 6: 2, 3, 15, 16, 19; 9: 13, 24, etc.

The kingdom is for the saints: Dan. 7: 18. Unsaintly conduct, therefore, as sure as it excludes from the church of God now, so surely will it exclude from the kingdom of God by-and-by: 1Cor. 5: 6.

In short, I trace in these words of the Holy Ghost a regular argument.
1. No unrighteous person shall enter the kingdom: ver. 9.
2. Some of you are unrighteous: ver. 8.
3. Therefore some of you shall not enter the kingdom.

(3) Eph. 5: 5. Is not the Epistle to the Ephesians addressed to believers? "To the saints which are at Ephesus, and to the faithful in Christ Jesus:" 1: 1. Paul, then, after describing their wondrous privileges as chosen in Christ, begs them to walk worthy of the call of God. He warns them first against obscene or light conversation, as unsuited to their profession: ver. 1-4. And if the talk about uncleanness was unsuitable, how much more the acting of it! He assures, therefore, the same persons, that to be guilty of such acts would exclude them from the kingdom. "For this ye know, * [* Or "know ye." As the Vulgate, and some critics.] that no whoremonger, or unclean person, or covetous man, who is an idolater, hath any inheritance in the kingdom of the Christ and God." Has no believer ever been guilty

of these sins? Are there no true believers in our day pressing on to 'make their fortune,' and esteeming themselves quite justified in doing wrong? Was no believer ever covetous? Or a lover of money? What says the Holy Ghost further? "Let no man deceive you with vain words: for because of these things cometh the wrath of God upon the children of disobedience. Be not ye therefore partakers with them:" ver. 6, 7. Is it not clear from this, that these offences were lightly regarded; and that believers were in danger of falling into them? But the wrath of God is coming upon these things: and God is no respecter of persons in judgment. If, then, it be found that believers partake in the world's sins, will they not partake of the judgment? Such, I suppose, is the apostle's meaning.

(4) Gal. 5: 19-21. In the believer the flesh still abides; can he not therefore fall into the lusts of the flesh? Yes: in point of doctrine and of fact it is certain that he may: 1 Cor. 5; 2Cor. 12: 20, 21. Then Paul by the Holy Ghost announces what are the works of the flesh; and adds, that those guilty of such deeds shall be excluded from the kingdom. In the next chapter he addresses the Galatian believers as "brethren:" ver. 1, 18. He warns them not to deceive themselves: and then adds, that the effects of our actions in the day to come will follow as surely as the reaping follows and depends upon the kind of the seed sown. "Be not deceived; God is not mocked: for whatsoever a man soweth, that shall he also reap. For he that soweth to his flesh shall (out) of

the flesh reap corruption; but he that soweth to the Spirit shall (out) of the Spirit reap life everlasting." [2] May not a believer sow to the flesh? Are not thousands of them doing so? Is not the sowing to the flesh the same as doing the works of the flesh? Then such - when the accepted enter the [millennial] kingdom - will be rejected.
(Robert Govett 2nd Letter To Molesworth: themillennialkingdom.org.uk)

JA Seiss
THE ADVENT AND THE CHURCH
I have not found a respectable or acknowledged creed in all Christendom, from the beginning until now, that teaches the doctrine of a millennium before Christ's coming. I have not found one single passage in all the Bible that sustains the doctrine of a millennium before Christ's coming. But, on the other hand, I have found a long and unbroken line of witnesses from the days of the Apostles until now, who testify with one voice that the hope of a millennium of universal righteousness, liberty, and peace before Christ comes, is a falsehood and a dream. I have found many eminent divines, who have blest the church and the world with their piety and wisdom, eagerly looking for the Savior's advent as the only thing that is to lift the church out of its present depression and gloom. And beyond and above all, I have found the Word of God everywhere pointing to the same great and glorious event as the only hope of the pious, and as the great link which alone can connect

us with or bring us into the joys and jubilations of the millennial era. Theorize and speculate as you please, when the Lord cometh He will find the world as now, full of vice, unbelief, sensuality and guilt. We may prefer our vague dreams, and set them up against God's positive revelations; but His truth abideth.

 Truth shall retire
Bestuck with slanderous darts, and works of faith
Rarely be found; so shall the world go on,
To good malignant, to bad men benign,
Under her own weight groaning, till the day
Appear, of reparation to the just,
And vengeance to the wicked, at return
Of Him - thy Saviour and thy Lord. - MILTON.

All through the New Testament the coming of the Lord is spoken of as an event that may occur at any day. From this alone, I know that we have no right to expect a millennium first. It is useless to tell me that it is only a providential, spiritual, figurative coming that is to occur before the millennium. Providentially, and spiritually, Christ is already here. Wherever two or three are gathered together in His name, there He is. He is now and ever at work in His providence, controlling, arranging, overruling, moving everything; and His Spirit* is given to every man to profit withal. Figuratively, He comes every day. Every meal we take, every breath we draw, every new pulsation of our life, He brings to us, as it were, by His own hand. And if His coming before the millennium includes no higher, no more real coming than these things amount to, then I know not upon what ground Christians can cope that He ever will return in person to our world. The Bible has no terms expressive of a literal and real coming, but those which describe His premillennial coming. When we read of the coming of other persons, we never think of allegory of figure. We take the language for what it means. Let us beware how we change the Holy Ghost with saying what He does mean. That servant who "says in his heart, My Lord delayeth His coming," the Saviour calls 'an evil servant.'

For if the Son of man should come this week, this month, or this year, would he find faith** on the earth? Would not the church itself be taken by surprise? Would not such an event now come upon the overwhelming majority of Christ's professed followers unawares? And yet, what guarantee have we that the chariot-wheels of the coming King are not already rumbling over the distant worlds? Has he not said, "In such an hour as ye think not the Son of man cometh"? "the day of the Lord so cometh as a thief in the night"? and "as a snare shall it come upon all them that dwell on the face of the whole earth"? Who can say that we are not liable to have the great scenes of the judgment precipitated upon us at any moment? And shall we not be concerned to have our minds familiarized with what may any day occur, and which must occur sooner or later? Is there not something inconceivably dreadful in

the thought of having that day come upon us at the very time we are saying, "My Lord delayeth His coming"? Would it not be better to be a little beforehand with our anticipations, and to bear the taunts that may be heaped upon us for our concern, than to accommodate ourselves to the wisdom and sobriety of this erring world, and be finally taken by surprise? Jesus says that the Lord of that servant who shall be found faithless, sleeping or scoffing, shall cut him asunder and appoint him his portion with the hypocrites, amid weeping and gnashing of teeth. "If the righteous scarcely be saved, where shall the ungodly and the sinner appear?" (1 Peter 4: 18). To this also agrees the account given in Matthew 24: 42-51; where we read of a servant who is 'faithful and wise,' whom his Lord finds at his post, and at once receives to blessedness; but also of another servant, as really a servant as the first, who is deficient in fidelity and worldly in his temper, and whom his Lord when He comes severely punishes by assigning him a portion with hypocrites, who are to suffer the great tribulation. The words do not all imply that the one is saved and the other is lost, but simply that the one reaches blessedness at once when the Lord comes, whilst the other, not being prepared by proper watchfulness, is 'left.' And punished with such temporal judgments as are then left to befall the earth, and only saved 'so as by fire' at the subsequent period.
(JA Seiss: The Advent and the Church; themillennialkingdom.org.uk)

Watchman Nee

"... those Christians who faithfully have followed the Lord shall enjoy glory a thousand years ahead of other Christians.... The second death is the lake of fire. Those who have no part in the first resurrection may yet be hurt by the second death. Some Christians will be disciplined in the future (see Matt. 18: 34, 35). He who wrongs his brother will be punished by the Lord (1Thess. 4.5, 6). We believers are exhorted to fear Him who has power to cast into hell... thus implying that OVER SOME CHRISTIANS HELL STILL HAS ITS THREAT (Luke 12: 4, 5). If a branch does not abide in Christ, he, like a branch, is liable to be cast off, withered, cast into the fire and burned (John 15.6).... Will there be anyone saved at the Great White Throne? The answer is yes.... The Bible explicitly states that those who do not confess Christ before men will not be confessed by Christ before the angels of God. This means they have no part in the kingdom. If they too were to appear at this juncture, they certainly should be among the saved."
(Watchman Nee, Come Lord Jesus (New York: Christian Fellowship Publishers, 1976), 212, 214-215, 221-222.)

Albert George Tilley

"Merit (or worthiness) it must be maintained in the teeth of all denial, is a condition and qualification for the First Resurrection...(Luke 20: 35).... Priests of God and Christ, they shall reign with him a thousand years... not instead of eternally, but Millennially before eternity proper begins. Others-proud, indulgent, cowardly-are

judged unworthy of Christ and of aeonian life. Now we know from several epistles that SOME BELIEVERS WILL BE EXCLUDED FROM THIS KINGDOM of Heaven and of God (Eph. 5: 5-8).… We are warned…' the rest of the dead (saved and unsaved) lived not again until the 1000 years were ended (Rev. 20: 5)… wicked and slothful servants being raised merely for the purpose of judgment, and then TEMPORARILY DISMISSED TO DARKNESS AND REMORSE IN THE HADES they were summoned from."
(A.G. Tilney, "Will All Believer's Share In The First Resurrection?," The Dawn (Nov. 15, 1938).

William Frederick Roadhouse
"But as we have before intimated, those not barred by the disqualifications that each of the Apostles and our Lord Jesus Christ clearly point out (as Galatians 5: 19-21, etc.) will have position and rulership in that coming Kingdom-those who 'suffer with Him' (2 Timothy 2: 12, Romans 8: 17); those who are counted 'worthy' (Luke 21: 36);…. A resurrection takes place. We remember that at the setting up of the rulership of the Overcomers, in chapter 20: 5, it was said, 'But the rest of the dead (believers) lived not again until the thousand years were finished.' They had won no crown. In Scriptural language, they had proven 'unworthy,' 'unfaithful'…. And hence they were not raised to 'reign with Him'…. God shake us up. When Revival comes we shall see this truth again! Let the reader remember these perfectly simple things-namely, no uncrowned

believer 'reigns with Christ,' and crowns are earned by sweat, labour, travail, even to death if need be."
(W.F. Roadhouse, Seeing The Revelation, (Toronto: The Overcomer Publishers, 1936), 221-222, 229-231.)

Robert Edward Neighbour
"It is easy to say that this evil servant in the parable [Matthew 25: 15-19] represents those in the church who are not saved, instead of the saved... The simple facts are these: First of all our Lord does not place His talents in the hand of the unregenerate; secondly, there are many among the truly saved who are hiding their talents in the earth... What then was the lot of the wicked and slothful servant?... In Matthew 25: 28 he loses his talent first of all, and then, in verse 30, he is said to be cast into OUTER DARKNESS, where there shall be weeping and gnashing of teeth... We shall receive for the BAD we have done. Now we hesitate. I hear no 'Amens!' Instead many begin to tremble... You ask at once—what will they receive?... Any child, properly reared, will tell you what he receives for bad behavior... He will say, 'a spanking.' Still you hesitate. You thought there could be no sorrow at the Judgment Seat of Christ. You thought there could be nothing by way of chastisement, and certainly nothing like weeping and gnashing of teeth. Then what did the Holy Spirit mean when Paul, after saying, that 'every one shall receive according to that which he hath done, whether it be ...bad,' added, 'knowing the terror of the Lord we persuade men.'... Think you that a just Judge will ignore

our unconfessed evil conduct?... Yes, the bad servants will be saved... but with no place in the kingdom... The parables of Christ plainly teach that the 'unprofitable' and 'wicked' and 'slothful' servant, shall have no place in the Kingdom....Remember Christ said, 'Not every one that saith unto me, Lord, Lord, shall enter into the Kingdom of heaven.' (Matthew 7: 21).... We believe in the security of the believer; we believe if you are born again, you can never be unborn ....However, the eternal security of a believer does not secure His rewards. Salvation is by grace, apart from works.... Salvation is the finished work of the Lord Jesus Christ.... All a sinner can do is to receive a finished and a completed work.... There has been, however, on the part of many who believe a grave error. They have turned away from many solemn warnings, which are plainly and positively written in the Word of God ....In our former sermon we emphasized that the land of Canaan was typical of the thousand year-reign of Christ, the millennial kingdom of our Lord. Of this heirship, the Book of Hebrews is constantly speaking. The Israelites were overthrown in the wilderness, and missed their heirship. Herein God has summed up the most solemn message in the Bible for saints upon whom the end of the age has come." (R.E. Neighbour, What Saith The Scriptures? (Ohio: Gems Of Gold), 73-74, 78-79, 107, 113-114, 116.)

G.F. Poynder

"This was the prize, 'the out-resurrection from amongst the dead' for which the Apostle Paul was striving, lest when he had preached to others, he himself should be a castaway, i.e. rejected at the judgment-seat of Christ for

the prize;.... This also was the prize for which the martyrs suffered themselves to be tortured, not accepting deliverance that they might obtain a better resurrection, that is, the first resurrection.... How important it is then for us to examine ourselves, and see whether we be in the faith.... And may we ever bear in mind the solemn warning contained in the judgment meted out to the wicked and unprofitable servant-His own bond-slave, entrusted with His Master's goods, and which had been more or less carefully preserved-'Thou wicked and slothful servant,-thou knewest... thou oughtest therefore... take the talent from him... and cast ye the unprofitable servant into outer darkness: there shall be weeping and gnashing of teeth'.... We may conclude that as he is his Lord's own bond-slave, bought with His own most precious Blood, entrusted with His goods, his name was entered in the Lamb's Book of Life... though he will of necessity have MISSED reigning with Christ in the Millennial Kingdom.... He immediately passes on to the account of the second or General Resurrection.... This separation and judgment must take place when the Great White Throne is set... those whose names are not written in the Lamb's Book of Life will be cast into the Lake of Fire; whilst those whose names are in that book, but were not judged to be worthy of the first resurrection, now enter into eternal life, so for them the Lord's promise as recorded in John 6: 39, 40, 44, 54, four times repeated, will be literally fulfilled... they will have everlasting life, being raised up as promised 'at the last day'.... But let it never be forgotten;-he will miss the prize, the first or better resurrection, the joy of entering the Marriage Feast, and living and reigning with his Lord during the Millennium." (Samuel Wilkinson, in the Foreword to Poynder's Judgment (Wooton, St. Lawrence, Church Grove, Fleet, Hants).

Dr Alfred Taylor Schofield: "... we are all perfectly clear that entrance into eternal life is of grace alone... but Scripture clearly shows that there are definite rewards and losses with regard to our Christian conduct in this world.... This is the point I would put definitely before you. For forty years I have glossed over every passage which refers to exclusion, and have refused to apply it to the Christian man. But on the face of them, these passages do apply to Christians everywhere. They are in Epistles written to Christians, and are safeguarded at the time, as applying to Christians. I feel that when an Apostle says, 'Be not deceived,' there may be great danger that some will be deceived, in applying Scriptures to other people and carefully shielding the application from ourselves. First, I would appeal to you, on those grounds, quietly to read those short passages which have been alluded to, many of them, over again....' Be not deceived.' Why that solemn warning? No one that is an unconverted adulterer will inherit the

kingdom of God. What class then could be deceived? Only Christians…. Does not the Apostle bring home to the consciences of Christians (not merely professors or clearly unconverted people to whom these words surely cannot apply), the fact that they shall not inherit the kingdom of God by which I here understood the Millennial Kingdom of Christ?"
(The Entrance Into The Kingdom Of God, Prophecy Investigation Society, Nov. 12th, 1909 (London), 31-32.)

Hudson Taylor

"The question is frequently asked, Who are represented by the daughters of Jerusalem? They are clearly not the bride, yet they are not far removed from her…. They have forgotten the warning of our LORD in Luke xxi. 34-36; and hence they are not 'accounted worthy to escape all these things that shall come to pass, and to stand before the SON of Man.' They have not, with Paul, counted 'all things but loss for the excellency of the knowledge of CHRIST JESUS the LORD,' and hence they do not 'attain unto' that resurrection from among the dead, which Paul felt he might miss, but aimed to attain unto. We wish to place on record our solemn conviction that not all who are Christians, or think themselves to be such, will attain to that resurrection of which St. Paul speaks in Phil. iii …"
(Hudson Taylor, Union And Communion With Christ (London: China Inland Mission, Ninth Impression, 1929), Appendix: "Daughters Of Jerusalem".)

Barnabus (A.D. 100):

"Let us be spiritually-minded: let us be a perfect temple to God. As much as in us lies, let us meditate upon the fear of God, and let us keep His commandments, that we may rejoice in His ordinances. The Lord will judge the world without respect of persons. Each will receive as he has done: if he is righteous, his righteousness will precede him; if he is wicked, the reward of wickedness is before him. Take heed, lest resting at our ease, as those who are the called [of God], we should fall asleep in our sins, and the wicked prince, acquiring power over us, should thrust us away from the kingdom of the Lord. And all the more attend to this, my brethren, when ye reflect and behold, that after so great signs and wonders were wrought in Israel, they were thus [at length] abandoned. Let us beware lest we be found [fulfilling that saying], as it is written, 'Many are called, but few are chosen ....Attend, my children, to the meaning of this expression, 'He finished in six days.' This implieth that the Lord will finish all things in six thousand years, for a day is with Him a thousand years. And He Himself testifieth saying, 'Behold, today will be as a thousand years.' Therefore, my children, in six days, that is, in six thousand years, all things will be finished. 'And He rested on the seventh day.' This meaneth: when His Son, coming [again], shall destroy the time of the wicked man, and judge the ungodly, and change the-sun, and the moon, and the stars, then shall He truly rest on the seventh day.... Thou shalt remember the day of judgment, night and day.... It is well,

therefore, that he who has learned the judgments of the Lord, as many as have been written, should walk in them. For he who keepeth these shall be glorified in the kingdom of God; but he who chooseth other things shall be destroyed with his works. On this account there will be a resurrection, on this account a retribution.....The Lord is near, and His reward."
(Coxe, A. Clevend, The Ante-Nicene Fathers (Grand Rapids: Wm. B. Eerdmans), The Epistle of Barnabas.)

Polycarp:
 "In whom, though now ye see Him not, ye believe, and believing, rejoice with joy unspeakable and full of glory; into which joy many desire to enter, knowing that 'by grace ye are saved, not of works,' but by the will of God through Jesus Christ.... But He who raised Him up from the dead will raise up us also, if we do His will, and walk in His commandments, and love what He loved, keeping ourselves from all unrighteousness, covetousness, love of money, evil speaking, false witness; 'not rendering evil for evil, or railing for railing,' or blow for blow, or cursing for cursing, but being mindful of what the Lord said in His teaching: 'Judge not, that ye be not judged; forgive, and it shall be forgiven unto you; be merciful, that ye may obtain mercy; with what measure ye mete, it shall be measured to you again; and once more, 'Blessed are the poor, and those that are persecuted for righteousness' sake, for theirs is the kingdom of God.'... Knowing, then, that 'God is not mocked,' we ought to walk worthy of His commandment and glory.... If we

please Him in this present world, we shall receive also the future world, according as He has promised to us that He will raise us again from the dead, and that if we live worthily of Him, 'we shall also reign together with Him,'... In like manner, let the young men also be blameless in all things, being especially careful to preserve purity, and keeping themselves in, as with a bridle, from every kind of evil. For it is well that they should be cut off from the lusts that are in the world, since 'every lust warreth against the spirit;' and 'neither fornicators, nor effeminate, nor abusers of themselves with mankind, shall inherit the kingdom of God,' nor those who do things inconsistent and unbecoming.... If then we entreat the Lord to forgive us, we ought also ourselves to forgive; for we are before the eyes of our Lord and God, and 'we must all appear at the judgment-seat of Christ, and must every one give an account of himself.' Let us then serve Him in fear, and with all reverence, even as He Himself has commanded us, and as the apostles who preached the Gospel unto us, and the prophets who proclaimed beforehand the coming of the Lord [have alike taught us]."
(The Epistle Of Polycarp To The Philippians (Albany, OR: Ages Digital Library Collections)

Apostle Paul

Galatians 5:16-21

[16] This I say then, Walk in the Spirit, and ye shall not fulfil the lust of the flesh.

[17] For the flesh lusteth against the Spirit, and the Spirit against the flesh: and these are contrary the one to the other: so that ye cannot do the things that ye would.

[18] But if ye be led of the Spirit, ye are not under the law.

[19] Now the works of the flesh are manifest, which are these; Adultery, fornication, uncleanness, lasciviousness,

[20] Idolatry, witchcraft, hatred, variance, emulations, wrath, strife, seditions, heresies,

[21] Envyings, murders, drunkenness, revellings, and such like: of the which I tell you before, as I have also told you in time past, that they which do such things shall not inherit the kingdom of God.

Jesus Christ

Matthew 7:13-23

13 Enter ye in at the strait gate: for wide is the gate, and broad is the way, that leadeth to destruction, and many there be which go in thereat:

14 Because strait is the gate, and narrow is the way, which leadeth unto life, and few there be that find it.

15 Beware of false prophets, which come to you in sheep's clothing, but inwardly they are ravening wolves.

16 Ye shall know them by their fruits. Do men gather grapes of thorns, or figs of thistles?

17 Even so every good tree bringeth forth good fruit; but a corrupt tree bringeth forth evil fruit.

18 A good tree cannot bring forth evil fruit, neither can a corrupt tree bring forth good fruit.

19 Every tree that bringeth not forth good fruit is hewn down, and cast into the fire.

20 Wherefore by their fruits ye shall know them.

21 Not every one that saith unto me, Lord, Lord, shall enter into the kingdom of heaven; but he that doeth the will of my Father which is in heaven.

22 Many will say to me in that day, Lord, Lord, have we not prophesied in thy name? and in thy name have cast out devils? and in thy name done many wonderful works?

23 And then will I profess unto them, I never knew you: depart from me, ye that work iniquity.

Kingdom Come is a Book written to address the concerns of the modern Charismatic Movement called the New Apostolic Reformation. (NAR) Kingdom Come is written to give a Biblical response to the prevailing theology with in the NAR movement called; "Dominion Theology." Many questions and concerns have arisen over the last several decades about the formation, doctrine and practices of the NAR movement. I have written Kingdom Come from the prospective of coming from the inside of the Charismatic Dominion theology camp. I will address the issue of modern day apostles and prophets and the formation of apostolic networks and Church government. I will also attempt to answer concerns of miracles, sings and wonders which help promote the NAR agenda.

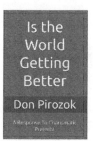

Now a debate has arisen between Christians who hold to coming dark days and an end time Tribulation, and the Charismatic Preterist's who believe that dark days have already passed. Of course, they both can't be true, as they are in 180 degrees in opposition one to the other. One is the invention of man; the other had been dene0loped bu hte authority of Scriputres. Here is the test question for both camps, does the Bible teach a catastiopohic ending to this age, or a golden age, a Christian worldwode utopia? Imagine the problems whih will arise for Charismatic Christians, who adopt and hold to the false views of end times which will be the complete opposite to what they teach and believe.